International Journal on Criminology

Volume 3, Number 2 • Fall 2015

Contents

PSO

International Journal on Criminology - Fall 2015, Volume 3, Number 2

The Cyclical Evolution of Homicides and Security

Maurice Cusson[A]

In a cycle, a series of events are repeated in the same order and return to their starting point. Between 1900 and 2013, homicide rates in Canada and the United States fluctuated as follows: 1) from 1900 to 1930, homicides soared, during a period of economic growth, social euphoria, an expanding organized crime and police corruption; 2) between 1931 and 1955, homicide rates declined during a period of severe economic recession, tight social controls and improvements in private and public security; 3) between 1956 and 1989, homicides skyrocketed during the postwar boom, while social controls were eased and the police became more bureaucratic; 4) as of 1990, homicide rates have fallen in a context of an ageing population and innovations in policing. The article ends by offering a general theory of crime rate cycle. The model rests on three hypotheses: that crime adapts to security and vice versa; that security excesses in one direction lead to excesses in the opposite direction; and that one phase in the cycle of crime is the cause of the phase that follows.

Keywords: *cycle, crime rates, security, homicides, organized crime, police, private security, corruption, social controls, cyclical theory.*

A cycle may be defined as an ongoing sequence of changes that follow one another in the same order as in the cycle of the seasons. In economics, no one disputes the existence of recurrent business cycles: a phase of growth is followed by a phase of recession, which begins with a crisis followed by a contraction and, lastly, the recovery that marks the beginning of a new cycle. Economists seek an explanation of one phase of a cycle in the preceding. A crisis is caused by the prosperity and frenetic speculation of the preceding phase. A growth spurt causes a crisis and then a recession.

Are there cycles of crime, with repeated sequences of periods of security and insecurity, order and disorder, alternating in a regular pattern? Examples of the cyclical development of crime are rare, but a few can be identified, like the evolution of homicides in New York City during the last two centuries.

Monkkonen (2001) finds three long waves in the New York City homicide rate between 1800 and 2000. The first peaked in 1864 after a lull between 1820 and 1830. The second came to a head in 1931 after a respite between 1890 and 1900, while the third was a tidal wave that hit the city with rates that reached an unprecedented height

[A] International Center for Comparative Criminology, Université de Montréal

doi: 10.18278/ijc.3.2.1

of 28 per 100,000 inhabitants in 1991. This was preceded by a respite of 5 per 100,000 around 1950. According to Monkkonen, tolerance for violence will push homicides up. Then comes a phase in which most citizens find the violence as intolerable, which will drive it down. After some time, the buildup of actions against violent crime bears fruit and the incidence of homicide begins to fall. When peace and security last too long, however, people see no reason to continue cracking down on violence. The subsequent easing up prepares the ground for another phase that will manifest itself in a fresh upsurge in homicides.

A Century of Murders in Canada and the United States

The fluctuations in the homicide rates in Canada and the United States display two distinctive features: the curves are in parallel and appear to be cyclical. The figure 1 shows a century of changing homicide rates in the United States and Canada (Ouimet 2008). With US rates four times higher than those of Canada, the respective scales are different, as the two sides of the graph show.

Figure 1: Changing Homicide Rates per 100,000 Inhabitants of Canada and the United States, 1901–2013 (Marc Ouimet)

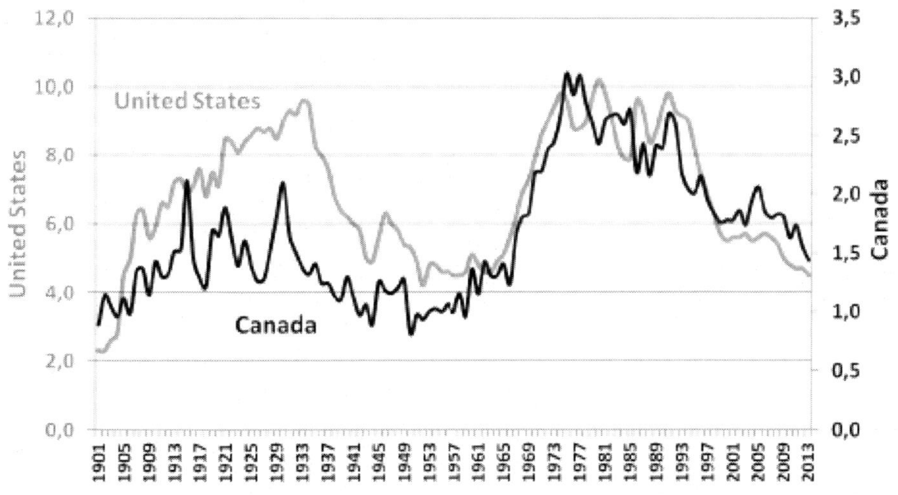

The homicide rates fluctuate in the same cyclical timing in both country and are remarkably in parallel, with the US scale three to four times higher than that of Canada. For each country, the figure shows an initial cycle beginning at the start of the century and ending in around 1960. This is followed by another cycle, which appears to be still ongoing at the time of writing. The figure can be divided into four phases: 1900–1930; 1931–1955; 1956–1989; and 1990–2013.

1900–1930: Homicide Growth, the Roaring Twenties, and Police Corruption

During this period, the United States recorded a homicide rate that rose from 2 per 100,000 inhabitants to 9 per 100,000. In the United States, historians use the term the "Progressive Era" for the first twenty years of the twentieth century. During that time, standards of living improved, the economy boomed, social reforms were introduced, and major technological advances were made, such as the automobile (Tindall and She 2004). Growing wealth and industrialization brought about the mass production of consumer goods, providing plenty of items for potential thieves to steal. Household incomes increased. People could afford to go out in the evening, drink alcohol, and have fun, which is known to be one of the features of a criminal lifestyle (Cusson 2005).

The next ten years, from 1920 to 1930, extended this earlier period as economic activity accelerated in an atmosphere of euphoria remembered as the "Roaring Twenties": a booming economy, the mass production of radios and cars. Sexual taboos were overturned. Divorce became increasingly common. Economic players on the financial markets were gripped by speculative fever.

In 1919, the prohibition movement in the United States drove federal lawmakers to pass an amendment to the Constitution, the Volstead Act, banning the manufacture, sale, and transport of alcoholic beverages. However, police officers enforced the law erratically, and were inclined to look the other way when offered bribes by the owners of drinking establishments. People continued to drink alcoholic beverages that were illegally produced and distributed by criminal gangs. Prohibition made the fortunes of the criminal gangs. Already thriving from running prostitution and gaming houses, these gangs underwent substantial expansion. Gang warfare bathed in blood a few major cities. In Chicago, Al Capone took control of the city's illegal breweries, distilleries, and drinking establishments. He also controlled prostitution, the gaming houses, and racketeering. Corrupt or intimidated, police officers and politicians left him to it (Kenney and Finckenauer 1995).

In Canada, as in the USA, the period between 1900 and 1929 was a time of economic expansion and prosperity. The country industrialized and urbanized. The rich became richer and spent lavishly.

The increase in the number of homicides at the time had nothing to do with poverty. On the contrary, this was a phase of economic expansion and social effervescence. If property crime was on the rise, it was because there were ever more consumer goods that could be stolen. People had the resources to go out and have fun in the evening. Some drank too much and became aggressive. Income from stealing enriched the underworld, which expanded.

In the US cities, police officers were hired through the influence of politicians or else bought their positions. Corruption reigned, and bribes ensured that police officers and their captains protected gaming houses, brothels, and illegal drinking establishments. When a citizen needed a police officer, there would be no one on duty. Lacking authority, the police chiefs of the day proved powerless to control their forces.

They could not recruit good candidates, rid themselves of the wildly incompetent, or crackdown on corruption (Fogelson 1977).

1931–1955: Decline in Homicide, Crash, and Recession

As of 1931 in Canada and 1933 in the United States, homicide rates declined drastically until 1942 to then remain at relatively low levels between 1943 and 1960.

The Great Depression of 1929 put a stop to the crazy years. The crash was followed by a long and harsh recession that lasted until 1942. Individuals' private incomes were in free fall, as was their purchasing power. Almost a quarter of the working-age population was unemployed. There were thirteen million unemployed in the United States in 1933 (Tindall and Shi 2004). The "New Deal" introduced a system of social protection, and the Welfare State came into being. In Canada, unemployment was rife, as it was in the United States, and salaries fell by 40 percent. Penury spread (Linteau, Durocher and Robert 1986).

As of 1939, under the pressure of the war raging in Europe, industries were mobilized to support the war effort. Full employment returned. Even so, the economic recovery did not translate into any tangible improvement of living standards, since resources were channeled into military production as a priority.

For nearly fifteen years (between 1930 and 1945), then, Canadians and Americans produced and purchased relatively few consumer goods, whether because of recession or the war economy. This meant that, during this period, would-be thieves had fairly few opportunities to make off with consumer durables. Teenagers and young adults could no longer afford to go out and have fun in the evening. Parents had no option but to stay in and look after their children.

In the United States, the criminal gangs that had called the shots in the 1920s were weakened by police operations and the end of prohibition. In Chicago, citizens, politicians, and honest police officers lost patience with Al Capone's celebrity status and his ostentatious display of power. Capone was declared "public enemy." In 1931, tax investigators managed to have Capone sentenced to eleven years in jail. In New York, one of the leading mafia bosses, "Lucky Luciano," found himself in police sights. He was arrested and sentenced to between thirty and fifty years in jail. He would be released during the war (Kenney and Finckenauer 1995). Such renewed police vigor, combined with the lifting of the prohibition laws, left US organized crime impoverished and disorganized.

On the police side, the unemployment brought about by the depression, surprisingly, helped improve recruitment of policemen. With restricted opportunities for work in trade and industry, a great many young people applied to be police officers. Candidates with little education or dubious morals were no longer hired. At the same time, police officers were better paid than before.

Between 1930 and 1955 in the United States and Canada, newspapers reported scandals in several city police forces, and journalists condemned corruption (Sherman

1978; Wadman and Allison 2004). In doing so, they echoed citizen groups that were calling for investigations. Under pressure from the resulting commissions of inquiry, the electoral system loosened its grip on police services. Corruption declined, although it still continued to exist.

It was at this time that private security became a force to be reckoned with. Americans had turned to the security market in response to the high crime rate that developed in the 1920s. In the United States, the number of private detectives is estimated to have gone from twenty thousand in 1920 to one hundred thousand in 1930. Over that same period, storekeepers and industrialists acquired better protection of their establishments and assets by resorting to watchmen, alarm systems, safes, and other security equipment (Fogelson 1977).

In short, the declining homicide rate of the 1930s and the recession of the 1940s and 1950s took place during a period of relative poverty, low consumption, tighter social controls, improved police personnel, vigorous police operations, weaker organized crime, and expanding private security.

1956–1989: The Growth of Crime in a Period of Economic Expansion

The homicide rates (but also the rates of most crimes for which there are reliable statistics) grew steadily from 1960 to 1975. They then remained high, and fluctuations were irregular. This growth in crime and its peak were seen not only in Canada and the United States but also in most Western countries. And it came about at a time of economic expansion: growing wealth and consumption, low unemployment. Purchasing power rose year after year. Mass production increased the number of targets likely to be of interest to thieves, particularly as electronic devices, were becoming lighter and easier to transport. The number of bank branches and convenience stores rose, offering targets to robbers. People increasingly traveled by car to go to work, to go out in the evening, to go away at the weekend, or on holiday. As a result, houses were left empty, a bargain for burglars. With plenty, came carelessness, and citizens protected themselves less and less well (Cohen and Felson 1979; Cusson 1990).

The population was younger, with a vast increase in the percentages aged fifteen to twenty-five, the age range known to be the most active in terms of offending. These young people became increasingly engaged in dissent and protest, particularly at the end of the 1960s and the beginning of the 1970s. Young adults, of whom there were simply too many, found it hard to find a foothold in the labor market.

Nearly everywhere in North America, police forces were caught off guard by a rising tide of crime. The bureaucratization of the police had reduced its adaptability, and the policing conception that held sway in the 1960s was missing the point. Police chiefs and officers were obsessed with the means and lost sight of the ends (Goldstein 1990). They relied on ineffective vehicle patrols. In United States inner cities, a gulf appeared between police officers and young Blacks.

The resemblance between the 1920s and the 1960s is striking. Those two periods—separated by forty years—of growth in partying and homicide were both periods of expansion: more wealth, more consumption, and, as a result, more goods vulnerable to theft and more money to spend on having a good time. Forty years apart, they were also periods of greater moral freedom, euphoria, optimism, and a weakening of informal social controls and policing.

1990–2013: Homicide Drop, Innovations in Policing and in Security Technology

In the 1990s and the first decade of the twenty-first century, homicides declined (at the time of writing, we do not know whether this drop will continue). During that time, Canadian homicide rates fell from 3 per 100,000 inhabitants in 1991 to 1.5 per 100,000 inhabitants in 2013. In the United States, the homicides drop from 9 per 100,000 inhabitants in 1991 to 4 in 2013.

These falls in homicides are part of the "crime drop." For a period of more than twenty years, many types of property and violent crime declined in several Western countries. This development led to a flurry of scientific studies (Blumstein and Wallman 2000, 2006; Ouimet 2004, 2005, 2008; Zimring 2007, 2012; Van Dijk 2008; Van Dijk et al. 2012; Aebi 2004; Aebi and Linde 2014; Tonry 2014; Farrell et al. 2014; Rosenfeld et al. 2007; Messner et al. 2007; Cusson 2010, 2015).

Rational choice theorists have an explanation for this crime drop. In reaction to the precedent growth of crime, security actors invested in situational crime prevention making crime more risky for offenders, more difficult, and less profitable (Felson 2002; Clarke 1983, 1995, 1997; Clarke and Newman 2006; Cusson 2010a, 2010b, 2015; Brantingham and Brantingham 1984; Van Dijk 2008, 2012; Ekblom 1999, 2004). This approach has been used to account for the drop in crime in New York, Canada, the United States as a whole, and England and Wales.

In New York City, moves against high levels of crime were instigated by Mayor Giuliani and his police chief, William Bratton, who concurred in making the fight against crime a priority (Silverman 1999). Zimring (2007, 2012) has shown that in New York City the actions that contributed most to declining crime were aggressive and proactive policing that targeted crime hot spots localized by the Comp Stat system. This strategy succeeded in driving down crime, especially gun homicide, in the targeted sectors (Rosenfeld et al. 2007; Messner et al. 2007).

At the same time, innovations and improvements within police organizations in Canada and the United States helped to reduce the crime rate of the 1990s and 2000s. State-of-the-art intelligence systems using computerized and increasingly well-analyzed databases enabled police officers to take more targeted action. Problem-oriented policing spread across North America, enabling police organizations to find tailor-made solutions, particularly in crime hot spots (Braga and Weisburd 2010). The impact of these policing innovations was to achieve a greater deterrent effect through more certain punishment, to disorganize and disarm criminal gangs, and to settle numerous interpersonal conflicts that might have escalated without police intervention (Cusson 2010, 2015).

During the 1980s and 1990s, a sharp increase in the quality and quantity of private security staff and security technologies exerted downward pressure on property crime (Cusson 2010). In the United States, security spending tripled during this time, while staff and security guards became more professional. Alarm systems proliferated and became more and more effective. Video-surveillance systems were installed in stores, banks, shopping malls, streets, warehouses, parking lots. Access-control systems helped monitor customers as they entered or left stores, banks, libraries, office blocks.

In England, Farrell et al. (2014) attributed the decline in burglaries since 1995 to the spread of household-protection systems, including sophisticated alarm systems, double-glazed windows with better locking devices, movement detectors, and security lighting. In the case of car thefts, they stressed more effective and widespread vehicle-security technologies, since 1993: central locking, alarms, electronic immobilizers, and tracking devices for tracing stolen vehicles. The upsurge in these security systems was closely followed by a drop in thefts in and of motor vehicles.

While technology and the security forces were cutting down opportunities for theft, the lifestyle of teenagers and young adults changed, bringing about a tightening of the family controls that had been eased in the preceding period. Indeed, during the exciting years from 1960 to 1980, young people went out in the evening to drink, dance, and fight. For some, theft had funded their party lifestyle. As of the 1990s, more and more young people were spending time at their computers, tablets, and video games. They became homebodies. Since they stayed inside most of the time, they had fewer opportunities to join a gang. This reconfiguration of lifestyles and social controls drove down burglaries, car thefts, and robberies, but cybercrime came into being.

In what follows, I intend to move to a more general level and, by building on what has gone before, to put forward a general theory of the crime rates cycles.

Hypotheses for a Theory of Crime Cycle

The model assumes that the most serious and best-measured crime categories tend to fluctuate in parallel. Indeed, in most Western countries, homicide, robbery with violence, and burglaries decline in the same years. This appears to mean that there are factors at work that apply to crime in general rather than specific factors that apply solely to individual categories of infraction. Three hypotheses help us understand the pattern of cyclical developments in crime and security.

A. Mutual adaptation. Offenders adapt to security measures and security officers adapt to crime. Thieves behave in an adapted fashion when they exploit a weakness such as poor locks. The incidence of thefts will fall if a response can be found—better locks, alarm systems, and so forth—until such time as the thieves find a way around the problem. On the other hand, rising crimes challenge security professionals so they seek solutions. By the same logic, during declining crime, the security operatives relax: Why worry about a problem already solved?

B. Security excesses in one direction lead to excesses in the opposite direction, resulting in alternations of too much and two little security. Too much crime generates excessive security responses, disregarding freedoms and human rights. By contrast, low crime rates encourage laxity, tolerance, and negligence.

C. One phase in a cycle is the cause of the next phase, so a phase may be explained by processes that began in the preceding phase. A period of rising crime is followed by a fall because, under pressure from too many crimes, security actors seek and find solutions.

The model proposed is close to the theory of responsive securitization (Van Dijk 2008, 2012). Van Dijk suggests that levels of victimization are determined by the interactions between the choices of the criminals and those of their victims. When the benefits of crime outweigh the costs, the number of offenders and offenses goes up. In response to growing costs to victims, the latter protect themselves, installing situational protection that will reduce the number of crime opportunities and, consequently, the number of crimes. Van Dijk conclusion: "Crime markets are equilibrium seeking."

The Four Phases of Crime and Security Cycle

I distinguish four successive phases in crime rates: 1) Growth; 2) Summit; 3) Decline; 4) Contraction. The phases follow on from one another, the reasons for one being found in the one before. After the fourth phase, the system goes back to the first.

I. Growth.

Crime begins to go up in times of abundance, partying, euphoria, and extravagance. Economic expansion pushes up purchasing power. With an abundance of goods and cash come opportunities for theft. People afford to have a good time and make the most of the opportunity. During a life as a party, alcohol, promiscuity, and excitements increase provocations and the risks of violent crimes (Cusson 2005). Nightlifers get into fights, indulge in excesses, and pay their debts from the fruits of stealing and trafficking. Criminal networks expand, and their members take control of drinking and other establishments. Gangs enter into competition with one another, resulting in bloody score settlings.

Growth in crime is self-sustaining. Rising profits from crime fund the party lifestyle of offenders and stimulate their criminal activity. Offenders devise new criminal tactics and find new gaps in the protection of goods and persons. Hoodlums have more and more opportunities to meet, spend time together, form networks, and organize. These more intense interactions stimulate repeat crimes: copycat crimes, differential associations, repeat victimizations, and revenge (Cusson 2008). One crime leads to another (Felson and Boba 2010).

Morals become laxer; tolerance, relativism, and insouciance are the order of the day. Goods are left unsupervised. The adults in authority are reluctant to take action. Young hoodlums have free rein and break the law with impunity. Judges and criminologists deny that there is a problem. Does crime really deserve to be punished? Is it not a social construct? Police becomes lax, legalistic, and bureaucratic. Police officers are corrupted.

Deprived of resources, the police staff is overwhelmed. This lead to a rise in the numbers of unsolved, unprosecuted, untried, and unpunished crimes.

2. Summit.

In phase 2, crime ceases to rise and remains high. An increase in crimes sets in motion a *critical-mass process*: activity is self-sustaining once the frequency of that activity passes a certain minimum level" (Schelling 1978). During this phase, however, there is increasing exasperation, and indignation at proliferating crime. The losses and suffering caused by so many crimes and offenses are felt more and more acutely, particularly in urban areas, where the worst crime is concentrated. Some clamor for harsher penalties. Nevertheless, responses are gradually discovered. Too much crime heightens the vigilance of security professionals. This paves the way to the next phase of the cycle.

3. Decline.

Crime declines with progress in security. In the Seventeenth and Eighteenth centuries France, the establishment of a powerful police organization was followed by a decline in homicides. In the first half of the nineteenth century, the creation of London's Metropolitan Police drove down crime. In Canada and the United States, the expansion of private security, with technological progress and the increased problem-solving ability of the police, cut crime in the last decade of the twentieth century (Cusson 2010).

Crime that is deemed excessive mobilizes citizens, police officers, and judges to make joint efforts to restore peace and tranquility. Victimizations and fear drive victims to protect themselves and take precautions. Ultimately, crime produces its own antibodies.

Once a decline is under way, it drives down repeat crimes and makes punishment more certain, because the law-enforcement agencies are no longer swamped. When a decline in crime begins, it is self-sustaining. Because there are fewer infractions, the process of repeat crimes slows down: fewer copycat crimes, fewer differential associations, and less repeat victimization. Less overwhelmed than before, police officers and judges find the time needed to solve problems.

Too much crime kills crime. Crime tends to concentrate in hot spots where it becomes so rife that, at the end, there is no victim or target to be found. Just as too many foxes eat so many hares that they cut off their own supply, too many very active criminals in a given area drive out storekeepers and asset owners. Those that do stay build their defenses and take extra precautions: before long, there will be little left to steal and few people to attack.

Crime devours its own children: in areas frequented by criminals, the examples of friends who are in jail, injured, destroyed by drugs, or murdered will act as a powerful deterrent to their younger peers and make parents more vigilant.

4. Contraction.

In phase 4, crime stabilizes at a relatively low floor. *Crime remains stable during a contraction because the security measures devised and implemented in preceding phases are still in place.* Prevention systems continue to provide protection and to deter potential offenders. Moreover, security professionals retain the expertise they have already gained.

However, all good things come to an end, and laxity sets in insidiously. There are insufficient incidents, offenses, and crimes to warrant vigilance. A good security system requires its professionals to be on the alert, but it becomes difficult to remain vigilant when nothing is happening: it's deadly dull. Private and public security experts face no challenges, their skills are lost, some shut themselves away in the legalism of bureaucracy, and others succumb to the temptations of corruption.

Security entails costs that seem increasingly prohibitive when crime is rare. Security does not come free of charge. There are the costs of a competent workforce and those of buying, installing, and maintaining security systems. Nonmonetary costs must be factored in as well: endless surveillance, stringent checks, locked doors, false alarms. All these waste time and are bothersome, irritating, and annoying. They earn scrupulous security officers a reputation as pernickety and intolerant.

With tolerance, people become more aware of the drawbacks, inconveniences, and dangers of "total security." When there are fewer victims of crime, intolerant and repressive attitudes cease to be appropriate. The call for security declines and is replaced by calls for compassion, people are more easily moved by the sufferings of prisoners than by those of their victims.

With fewer crimes, the cost-benefit ratio of security drops. There is a reluctance to pay for personnel to twiddle their thumbs or for equipment that seems no longer needed. Security seems detrimental to liberty. Encroachments into private life are criticized. Checks and searches at airports and elsewhere become exasperating. The specter of the "police state" is raised. Security loses its edge precisely because security has prevailed. So the conditions for a new growth in crime are reestablished and we return to the first phase or the cycle.

References

Aebi, Marcelo. 2004. "Crime Trends in Western Europe from the 1992 to 2000." *European Journal of Criminal Policy and Research* 10: 163–186.

Aebi, Marcelo, and Antonia Linde. 2014. "The Persistence of Lifestyles: Rates and Correlates of Homicides in Western Europe from 1960 to 2010." *European Journal of Criminology* 11: 552.

Blumstein, Alfred, and Joel Wallman, eds. 2000. *The Crime Drop in America*. Cambridge: Cambridge University Press. (Revised edition: 2006.) Braga, Anthony, and David Weisburd. 2010. *Policing Problem Places*. Oxford: Oxford University Press.

Brantingham, Paul J., and Patricia L. Brantingham. 1984. *Patterns in Crime*. New York: Macmillan.

Clarke, Ronald V. 1983. "Situational Crime Prevention: Its Theoretical Basis and Practical Scope." In *Crime and Justice: A Review of Research, Volume 4*, edited by Michael Tonry and Norval Morris, 225–56. Chicago: University of Chicago Press.

———, ed. 1997. *Situational Crime Prevention: Successful Case Studies*. 2nd ed. Guilderland, NY: Harrow and Heston.

Clarke, Ronald V., and Graeme R. Newman. 2006. *Outsmarting the Terrorists*. Westport, CT: Praeger Security International.

Cohen, Lawrence E., and Marcus Felson. 1979. "Social Change and Crime Rates." *American Sociological Review* 44: 588–608.

Cusson, Maurice. 1990. *Croissance et décroissance du crime*. Paris: Presses Universitaires de France.

———. 2005. *La Délinquance, une vie choisie*. Montreal: Hurtubise HMH.

———. 2008. "Répétitions criminelles, renseignements et opérations coup-de-poing." *Problèmes actuels de science criminelle*. Vol. XXI. Aix-en-Provence: Presses universitaires d'Aix-Marseille. Institut de sciences pénales et de criminologie.

———. 2010a. *L'Art de la sécurité*. Montreal: Hurtubise.

———. 2010b. "Dissuasion, justice et communication pénale." I*nstitut pour la justice, études et analyses*. www.publications-justice.fr

———. 2015. *Les homicides*. Montreal: Hurtubise.

Ekblom, Paul. 1999. "Can We Make Crime Prevention Adaptive by Learning from Other Evolutionary Struggles?" *Studies on Crime and Crime Prevention* 8: 27–51.

———. 2004. "How to Police the Future: Scanning for Scientific and Technological Innovations which Generate Potential Threats and Opportunities in Crime, Policing, and Crime Reduction." In *Crime Science: New Approaches to Preventing and Detecting Crime*, edited by Melissa Smith and Nick Tilley. Cullompton, UK: Willan.

Farrell, Graeme, Nick Tilley, and Andromachi Tseloni. 2014. "Why the Crime Drop?" *In Crime and Justice: A Review of Research*, Volume 43, edited by Michael Tonry, 421–90. Chicago: Chicago University Press.

Felson, Marcus. 1998. *Crime and Everyday Life*. 2nd ed. Thousand Oaks, CA: Pine Forge Press. (3rd edition: Thousand Oaks, CA: Sage, 2002.)

Felson, M. 2006. *Crime and Nature*. Thousand Oaks, CA: Sage.

Felson, M. and Boba, R. 2010. *Crime and Everyday Life*. Fourth ed. Thousand Oaks, CA: Pine Forge Press.

Fogelson, Robert M. 1977. *Big-City Police*. Cambridge MA: Harvard University Press.

Goldstein, Herman. 1990. *Problem-Oriented Policing*. New York: McGraw-Hill.

Kenney, Dennis Jay, and James O. Finckenauer. 1995. *Organized Crime in America*. Belmont, CA.: Wadsworth.

Killias, Martin. 2001. *Précis de criminologie*. 2nd ed. Bern, Switzerland: Staempfli. Linteau, Paul-André, René Durocher, and Jean-Claude Robert. 1986. *Histoire du Québec contemporain*. Montreal: Boréal Express.

Messner, Steven F., Sandro Galea, Kenneth J. Tardiff, Melissa Tracy, Angela Bucciarelli, Tinka Markham Piper, Victoria Frye, and Eric Henry Monkkonen. 1992. "History of Urban Police." In *Crime and Justice: A Review of Research, Volume 15*, edited by Michael Tonry and Norval Morris, 547–80. Chicago: The University of Chicago Press.

Monkkonen, Eric Henry. 2001. *Murder in New York City*. Berkeley, CA: University of California Press.

National Commission on Terrorist Attacks upon the United States. 2004. The *9/11 Commission Report*. New York: Norton.

Ouimet, Marc. 2004. "Oh Canada! La baisse de la criminalité au Canada et aux États-Unis entre 1991 et 2002." *Champ Pénal: Nouvelle Revue Française de Criminologie* 1. http:/champpenal.revues.org/

———. 2005. *La criminalité au Québec durant le vingtième siècle.* Quebec: les Presses de l'Université Laval.

———. 2008. "Crime and Crime Trends in Canada and the United States." In *Canada and the United States: Differences that Count*, edited by David M. Thomas and Barbar Boyle Torrey, 253–70. Toronto: Broadview Press.

Rosenfeld, Richard, Robert Fornango, and Andres F. Renfigo. 2007. "The Impact of Order-Maintenance Policing on New York City Homicide and Robbery Rates; 1988–2001." *Criminology* 45 (2): 355–84.

Tonry, Michael. 2014. "Why Crime Rates Are Falling throughout the Western World." In *Crime and Justice: A Review of Research, Volume 43*, edited by Michael Tonry, 1–63. Chicago: University of Chicago Press.

Schelling, Thomas. 1978. *Micromotives and Macrobehavior.* New York: Norton.

Sherman, Lawrence W. 1978. *Scandal and Reform: Controlling Police Corruption.* Berkeley, CA: University of California Press.

Spelman, William. 2000. "The Limited Importance of Prison Expansion." In *The Crime Drop in America*, edited by Alfred Blumstein and Joel Wallman, 97–129. Cambridge: Cambridge University Press. (Revised edition: 2006.)

Tindall, George Brown, and David Emory Shi. 2004. *America: A Narrative History.* New York: Norton.

Van Dijk, Jan. 2008. *The World of Crime.* Thousand Oaks, CA: Sage.

———. 2012. "Closing the Doors." Prizewinners Lecture, Stockholm Prize in Criminology.

———, Andromachi Tseloni, and Graham Farrell. 2012. *The International Crime Drop: New Directions in Research.* Basingstoke, UK: Palgrave Macmillan.

Wadman, Robert C., and William Thomas Allison. 2004. *To Protect and To Serve: A History of Police in America.* Upper Saddle River, NJ: Prentice Hall.

Zimring, Franklin E. 2007. *The Great American Crime Decline*. Oxford: Oxford University Press.

———. 2012. *The City that Became Safe*. Oxford: Oxford University Press.

Terrorism(s), Intelligence, and Freedoms: France's Patriot Act Light?

Alain Bauer[A]

In the 1970s, the then interior minister, Raymond Marcellin, had a hunch that terrorism would become a major challenge. This led him to summon the head of the domestic intelligence agency, the Directorate of Territorial Surveillance (Direction de la Surveillance du Territoire; DST), and recommend that he set up a specialist terrorism unit. Taken aback—shocked, even—at being thus "distracted" from his vital work of counterespionage, the chief "let it slip his mind." Marcellin, a Breton and typically stubborn, went ahead and simply ordered the unit into existence. The first modern reform of domestic intelligence was undertaken in 1990 at the instigation of the then prime minister, Michel Rocard, and his advisor, Prefect Rémy Pautrat, himself a former head of the DST. Nicolas Sarkozy set up the Central Directorate of Internal Intelligence (Direction centrale du renseignement intérieur; DCRI) and the Parliamentary Delegation for Intelligence between 2007 and 2012. A further step towards adopting relevant legislation was taken at the behest of interior minister Manuel Valls and Jean-Jacques Urvoas, chairman of the National Assembly Law Commission.

Once Valls had been moved to the prime minister's office at Matignon, the pair decided to add the finishing touches to this slow but tangible process by delivering modern legislation on intelligence that would be appropriate to the threats and technologies that had emerged since the fall of the Berlin Wall and the 2001 attacks.

The draft, which was of a very high standard, states that

> the intelligence services research, gather, exploit, and make available to the government information relating to geopolitical and strategic challenges and to threats and risks likely to affect the life of the nation. They facilitate awareness and anticipation of these challenges as well as the prevention and reduction of these risks and threats.

The text sets out seven ultimate purposes for which the intelligence services would be able to apply sometimes exceptional investigative techniques:

- national security (national independence, territorial integrity, and national defense, together with the prevention of any form of foreign intervention or attacks on the republican system or the stability of institutions);

[A] Professor of criminology at the National Conservatory for Arts and Crafts, New York and Beijing. Most recent work: *Qui est l'ennemi?*, CNRS Editions.

doi: 10.18278/ijc.3.2.2

- vital foreign policy interests and compliance with France's European and international commitments;
- France's vital economic and scientific interests;
- the prevention of terrorism;
- the prevention of the reformation or continuation of any previously dissolved groups;
- the prevention of organized crime and delinquency;
- the prevention of collective violence likely to result in serious disturbance of the public peace.

Six specialist intelligence services that may employ in a legal and controlled fashion highly intrusive measures to carry out their assigned tasks are identified: the General Directorate for External Security (Direction générale de la Sécurité extérieure; DGSE); the Defense Protection and Security Directorate (Direction de la Protection et de la Sécurité de la Défense; DPSD); the Military Intelligence Directorate (Direction du renseignement militaire; DRM), answerable to the Defense Ministry; the General Directorate for Internal Security (Direction générale de la sécurité intérieure; DGSI) at the Interior Ministry; and the National Directorate of Intelligence and Customs Investigations (Direction Nationale du Renseignement et des Enquêtes Douanières; DNRED) and Intelligence Processing and Action against Illegal Financial Networks (Traitement du renseignement et action contre les circuits financiers clandestins; TRACFIN) at the Economy Ministry.

I will not be reexamining here the details of what is a particularly detailed bill that will no doubt be fiercely debated in parliament. Rather, I will look at where further technical or legal improvements might be made.

Throughout the world, there is an intelligence community that is experiencing the same symptoms that can be observed in France. The first such intelligence community was set up in the United States in December 1981 by a Ronald Reagan irritated by the pointless and childish competition prevailing in the world of espionage. It brought together seventeen services (there are thought to have been more than 1,200 in the United States) from various ministries (for example, defense, security, justice, and energy) under the authority of the director of intelligence (who took office only in 2004).

In France, the 2008 White Paper would insist on the need to reform the Interministerial Intelligence Committee, founded in 1962 but largely underused despite an initial dusting off required by Michel Rocard in 1990.

In May 2011 and again in 2014, the prime minister set up an intelligence community (to be called special services) that defined the sector's "first division." It includes military agencies (the DGSE, DPSD, and DRM), a police service (the DCRI, which has since become the DGSI) and two services subordinate to the Economy Ministry (the DNRED and TRACFIN). The latter was better known as an analysis service; its inclusion in the list owes as much to the need for an overall balance between civilian and military agencies as it does to the standard of its services, which are considered outstanding.

Domestic intelligence does not feature (the Central Directorate of General Intelligence having vanished with the birth of the DCRI); the Gendarmerie is passed over (it made great efforts not to be included in the sector and continues to pay the price for its squeamishness, despite the existence of a Subdirectorate of Advance Operational Information [Sous Direction de l'anticipation opérationnelle; SDAO], about which one might quite properly ask whether it is not in fact an intelligence service) and is squabbling about prison intelligence (even though there are constant reminders that it is a crucial issue). The potential role of municipal police services has been overlooked (even though they "belong to the locality," while private operators, especially on public transport and at big stores, usually keep their eyes peeled).

And while the creation of a national intelligence coordinator seems like substantial progress, the special services community remains very small, since intelligence gathering, analysis, interception, and response are often combined.

The main room for progress, then, is in respect of the community itself, which would be better defined by abandoning the notion that it should be singular when its focus is plural.

What in fact exists is an intelligence-gathering community that has to embrace domestic police intelligence, the Gendarmerie's provision of advance operational information, prison intelligence, municipal police officers, and security operatives from the big public- and private-service operators (for example, postal services and transport), all of which are able to act as the eyes and ears of the nation.

Certainly, there is no need for any great change to the list of action-focused special services. However, between the extended circumference and the still small center, there is room for something essential and still very tenuous—a space for analysis.

Recruitment, training, and updating efforts have been announced and in some cases set in motion. The general rationale has not yet been sufficiently addressed, however.

A multitude of systems blithely compiles, still rarely trades, and applies the precautionary principle to drawing up ever fuller and less selective lists, making it possible to add to the use of belts, straps, and parachutes in seeking to avoid the risk of error. As it loses sight of what is essential and what is not, however, the system lays great stress on calling in particular for more resources. It reasons, as is often the way in these cases, that the burglar got away because the police station needed renovating. This does not mean that there is no need for better (and maybe even more) resources but, above all, that the process of change set in motion with the creation of the DCRI and its metamorphosis into the DGSI must be accepted and accelerated.

Whatever the formula that makes it possible to bring together all those who defend and protect the country so as to expand intelligence gathering and share its analysis in a process under the authority of the General Directorate of the National Police (Direction générale de la Police nationale; DGPN), the DGSI, and the DGPN, it will have to assert the existence of a General Intelligence Staff, dictated by circumstance and the will of the interior minister. For if there is a war, it will have to be well managed.

Beyond this key problem, it remains to be seen to what extent the National Commission for Control of Intelligence Techniques (Commission nationale de contrôle des techniques de renseignement; CNCTR) that has been established will be able to act given that it is rather small in composition and not open to persons with anything other than engineering qualifications. It is possible to defend basic rights while respecting the confidentiality of deliberations.

Jean Marie Delarue, incumbent president of the National Commission for the Control of Security Interceptions (Commission nationale de contrôle des interceptions de sécurité; CNCIS), offered some fairly harsh criticism that was reported by AEF Infos: "The draft law on intelligence is not compatible with public freedoms or with the security of the country. Thought must be given to comprehensive amendment of this document which, as it stands, merits severe criticism." Delarue describes the future body as a "colossus with feet of clay. This draft law does not respect the conditions for effective control." The state councilor is also worried about the data collection technologies introduced by the bill, which are clearly reminiscent of "dragnet techniques."

The idea of investing the Council of State with the relevant authority to "inquire into the implementation of intelligence techniques" and to have it rule "in the first and last instance" on disputes about intelligence "through specialist training" makes perfect sense. The institution has proven its ability to defend individual and collective freedoms. There is still a question mark regarding the lack of any legal officer to authorize dispensatory, exceptional, and fast-track procedures.

In fact, at least one service continues to have a judicial remit (the DGSI), while terrorism as an organized crime still falls within that of the judicial authorities. In addition, since 1986, efficient and effective machinery that cannot be suspected of complacency has been established (antiterrorism judges and the Antiterrorist Section of the Prosecutor's Office). One might legitimately wonder, therefore, why the government continues (the website-prohibition text was put together in precisely the same way at the end of 2014) not to invoke a legal officer who could be established as a national point of reference that is able to legitimize exceptionally intrusive measures in exceptionally serious circumstances—and to enable construction of a case that holds up in court without the use of timely anonymous reports or protected informers.

Numerous people will take fright at a document that nevertheless enables the regulation of intelligence procedures. It is a useful, brave, and fairly balanced move, weakened, paradoxically, by the lack of a judge offering protection in the most intrusive sector. We have already seen how difficult it has been to handle irregular or illegal intelligence in the context of never-ending legal proceedings and occasionally creative jurisprudence.

Parliament has an opportunity to take charge of this, and the Constitutional Council can give its opinion one way or another. There is room for the bill to advance.

The document's rapporteurs and the government are too astute to dispense with a more balanced but equally effective process.

Organized Crime Behind Bars

François Haut[A]

INTRODUCTION

While the Charlie Hebdo attacks in Paris in January 2015 unsurprisingly erased the memory of the previous evening, when television viewers[1] had seen how the inmates of Baumettes prison were posting their exploits on Facebook[2] flourishing drugs and wads of cash, they also seem to have made people forget just as quickly that these attacks only occurred because of serious societal shortcomings—most notably that the perpetrators had been radicalized, specifically, in prison.

Prison crime may be considered as one of the protagonists in what has been termed the "Contemporary Criminal Menace." In France it is equally as serious as other forms of organized criminal activity, with one difference—the subject is simply not discussed. It is taboo. Yet another "French exception" that seems to have rendered the current Minister of Justice (among others) willfully ignorant, leading her to declare before the Law Commission of the National Assembly[3] that it was "not desirable to share criminal information from prisons with the intelligence community."

She is undoubtedly right. How, after all, could it possibly be useful to know precisely what is happening in our prisons or to cross-check this information? It's a well-known fact that nothing really happens inside, well, no real wrongdoing... It's also undoubtedly why Rédoine Faïd, a robber arrested in June 2011 and who claimed to have become a reformed character, escaped from Lille-Sequedin prison on April 13, 2013, less than two years later, using "only" handguns and explosives and taking "only" four guards as hostages.

The images of his escape were made public, much to the dismay of prison officers "shocked" by their broadcast on TV channels M6 and TF1. The Justice Minister, Christiane Taubira "questioned" and expressed "concern" over video footage "highlighting criminal acts likely to undermine the dignity of prison staff," forgetting, perhaps, that a number of serious questions remain unanswered.

Is France soon to witness criminal acts comparable to those we have watched unfold in the United States in recent times?

[A] Head of the Department for Research into Contemporary Criminal Threats, Université Panthéon-Assas, Paris

[1] BFM TV, January 6, 2015 https://www.youtube.com/watch?v=ugkBXt6iCpE

[2] Facebook account *MDR o Baumettes* ("Baumettes lol").

[3] March 31, 2015

doi: 10.18278/ijc.3.2.3

On October 7, 2008, Texas Senator John Whitmire, chairman of the Senate Committee on Criminal Justice, received a call which, he said later, "made me horribly afraid." "I know the names of your daughters, a voice said to him, I know how old they are; I know where they live." The voice went on to provide precisely that information—their surnames, first names and addresses.

The person who uttered these phone threats was at least a double, and probably four-time murderer. He was at the time in a Death Row cell in Polunsky Prison,[4] southern Texas. He was in theory under close guard, yet Richard Tabler had managed to terrify one of the most powerful politicians in the state using a smuggled mobile phone.[5]

Among the panoply of contemporary criminal threats, one is particularly insidious and unappreciated, and that is the crime that abounds within prison walls.

The laws of all countries provide for the deprivation of physical liberty for specific reasons, with penalties to be served in prisons.[6] These custodial sentences[7] serve to punish and correct the convicted person if possible and prevent them from further harming society. Yet in prisons around the world, we see astonishing events unfold, and ever more frequently. We see elaborate trafficking, bloody battles; individuals already imprisoned for many years being tried and convicted anew, inside.

A general trend towards leniency and compassion, often in the name of atonement, has led to the establishment of spaces of freedom, both intellectual and physical, inside prisons, in the cells and the common areas. Thus, we see prisoners studying, for example, an activity that is perfectly aligned with one of the stated purposes of sentencing. Others, however, take maximum advantage of this generosity. The general increase in prison population density generates a promiscuity which complicates surveillance and control, while the increasingly collective nature of crime predisposes the prison population to coalesce into groups.

In prisons, the natural propensity of individuals to congregate together is enhanced. Where survival in a closed environment requires both discretion and a capacity to react to immediate violence, it also calls for gregarious cohesion and discipline. These skills develop according to the pace of life and with time. Each day allows the inmate to adapt to the environment and its repressive mechanisms. "Prisoners have twenty-four hours a day to figure out how to beat the system," as one prison administrative official has remarked.[8]

---

[4] Southwest of Livingston, Texas.

[5] Beiser, Vince. "Prisoners Run Gangs, Plan Escapes and Even Order Hits with Smuggled Cellphones." *Wired*, May 22, 2009.

[6] According to a generic terminology: Guinchard Serge and Thierry Debard. *Lexique des termes juridiques, 14th edition*. Paris: Dalloz, 2003, 457.

[7] Decoq, André. *Droit pénal général*. Paris: A. Colin, 1971, 380.

[8] Brian Parry, Deputy Director of the California Prison Administration, quoted by the Santa Rosa Press Democrat, April 24, 2001.

The conditions are reinforced by a general lack of commodities and services, a situation which confers a disproportionate level of power upon those in a position to satisfy these needs.

Thus we see, in almost all prisons around the world, groups which often transform into genuine criminal power structures, either created inside, often under the guise of self-protection, or having been re-established on the foundations of prior membership of criminal organizations. They may also come together around religious proselytism with activist aims.[9]

Elaborate organizational structures gradually divert the penitentiary purpose to serve their own ends and, through a perverse logic, also extend their capacity for harm outwards, beyond the prison walls. These organizations, ubiquitous and comparable, are indicative of a deep, little-known and poorly accepted dysfunction—one in which the triple function of the deprivation of liberty is no longer served.

These organizations, which are a particular form of organized crime, belong to what have been called the "protagonists" of the Contemporary Criminal Threat. They constitute a specific criminal threat, which challenges the effectiveness of the sentence, and thus our penal philosophy as a whole: it has been dubbed the "Threat of Prison Criminality." It raises a legitimate concern and calls for serious study.

We intend to show here the extent of the phenomenon, using significant examples. We shall develop an understanding of the principles generally implemented in the establishment and functioning of these entities. We shall also examine the damage, the pathogenesis of this threat of prison criminality in society at large.

I - SYMPTOMATOLOGY OF PRISON CRIMINALITY

A worldwide, contemporary, and expanding phenomenon, the threat of prison criminality is not some immaterial notion. It is constituted of people and the organizations they have created. It is therefore necessary to conduct a symptomatic approach in the first instance which, without being exhaustive, will reveal the existence of the threat and its brutal reality.[10] We shall note that most often we are dealing with identifiable associations, created within the prison world, or re-establishing themselves inside and putting down roots there. They distort the meaning of the prison sentence and disrupt the normal functioning of the institution, within which and beyond which these groups conduct criminal activities of all kinds.[11] These organizations have been called "Criminal Prison Gangs."

[9] Research into this particular phenomenon, now known by the name of Prislam (Prison-Islam) in the United States, but which can be found elsewhere, merits a specific study. It will only be referred to here through some symptomatic epiphenomena.

[10] While the study of criminal societies may sometimes be based on observation, this is rarely possible in the prison world. We must therefore rely on documents, the veracity of which is not always possible to ascertain, even though many are sworn statements; others, coincidentally, are revealing.

[11] The California prison administration gives a definition of Prison Gangs as "Any association or group of three or more people who share a name, sign or identification symbol, and whose members or

A - France: an Exception or Willful Ignorance?

In March 2015, an inmate escaped from the semi-open quarters of Baumettes prison by climbing over the fence. He escaped from the precinct but was still within the confines of the prison perimeter. It is thought he was on a mission to retrieve a package sent from outside. Another prisoner filmed the scene with his mobile phone…

Elsewhere, on November 18, 2013, a guard at Pontet prison near Avignon called the *gendarmes* from his watchtower after spotting two men near the perimeter wall. The men, one aged seventeen and the other twenty-two, were arrested. The first, who had crossed the barbed wire fence, told the gendarmes he had already thrown seven parcels over the fences for prisoners out exercising.

For the most part these packages contained alcohol. Near the second, the police found a number of plastic bags in the grass. They contained fifty-two packages in all, waiting to be sent over the fence. In them were several mobile phones, 100 grams of cannabis, screwdriver tips, one wrench, alcohol, and some meat, among other things.

This is not an isolated incident, and the problem takes various forms. In March 2003 a car theft ring, called "extensive" by police involved in the investigation, was organized and led by a criminal boss at the time incarcerated in Saint-Quentin-Fallavier prison (Isère, France).[12] Stretching as far as Marseilles, activities included homejackings[13] and carjackings.[14] These were carried out by gang members from the roughest no-go areas of Grenoble turning to serious organized crime.[15] Although behind bars, the gang's boss was running this large-scale gang operation smoothly from his cell using a mobile phone, a situation familiar to prison staff in many countries of the world,[16] and which in France is undoubtedly neither an exception, nor this a unique case.

The prevalence of mobile phones in French prisons no longer surprises anyone. For example, on February 12, 2004, in response to persistent rumors of the existence of a loose firearm in a prison at Nanterre, a systematic search succeeded in finding no fewer than fifteen mobile phones.[17]

---

associates practice or have practiced individually or collectively on behalf of the association or group, two or more acts including preparation, organization, threats, financing, illegal acts or acts of rebellion described as serious in accordance with Section 3315 of the California Code of Regulations."

[12] "Le Figaro", March 20, 2003.

[13] In French, "*Saucissonage*"—the act of entering a home against the will of its occupants and extracting property, valuables or actions under threat and/or violence—in this case vehicle keys.

[14] Taking an occupied vehicle by violent means.

[15] As for all criminal activities, again, we can only consider those for which there is prima facie evidence—which are known and therefore have been discovered. For that reason they have probably been stopped, sometimes even brought to justice. This in no way signifies that similar activities—and others—are not ongoing in the same places or elsewhere. All indications rather suggest that there has been an increase and diversification of criminal activity in prisons.

[16] For example Beiser. *Prisoners Run Gangs...*

[17] *Le Parisien*, February 13, 2004.

According to Bruno Hauron, deputy assistant to the chief of security in the prison system management at the time, "the mobile phone is, above all, an extremely useful tool in planning an escape—in the past, prisoners sent letters with coded messages, or signals from the prison windows to their accomplices outside. With a mobile phone, they can instruct the getaway motorcyclist waiting at a certain place, report their position within the prison, or order tools to be delivered to them."[18]

The use made of the mobile phone in Saint-Quentin-Fallavier and in many other prisons, reveals a far more serious problem—that at least one organized entity, and maybe others in other French prisons, are working from within the custodial system and radiating to the outside world. According to the staff cited above, the organization must have benefited from internal complicity obtained, as one might fear, through corruption and threats.

The dismantling of a drug trafficking ring in Marseilles and Salon-de-Provence, announced on September 30, 2009, found that it had been directed from inside the Baumettes prison. This was also the conclusion reached by the judge during the trial of another drug trafficking organization in the 15th *arrondissement* of Marseilles, which ended on September 28 of that same year. Once again, operations were directed from prison using mobile phones.[19]

For one former prisoner, Abdel Hafed Benotman, author of two books on his time inside, corruption is rife in French prisons. "In a lot of jails there are teams of two or three prison guards operating more or less like gangs in uniform. They start off very simply, with a light touch, putting out feelers and slowly but surely building links and contact networks... Others are in it for the fascination inspired by the biggest gangsters inside. They can hand out any number of sweeteners—free girls and booze are always on tap for the right guys in the bars and clubs they own."[20] This, at least, is the story that transpired from the case of two guards from the Ajaccio custodial center, convicted in 2003, and who, according to the Public Prosecutor of South Corsica[21] had been involved in "organized corruption."

Now, where there is "corruption" there is also the corruptor, and the "organized" nature of the said corruption implies the existence of organized groups in at least two French prisons. When the escapes we have already spoken of are taken into account, prepared as they were with care, clearly employing the necessary means, connections and close coordination between internal and external agents, the conclusions that follow are inescapable.

On October 9, 2004, "*Le Gominé*" a notorious gangster imprisoned at La Santé prison, escaped from a clinic in Paris where he had been taken for a medical examination. Le Gominé is an armed robber whom DNA tests have also implicated in a number of rapes. In early September, a police officer who interviewed him with

[18] *Le Figaro*, February 2, 2004.

[19] Trossero, Denis. *La Provence*, October 3, 2009.

[20] *Le Figaro*, February 2, 2004.

[21] *Libération*, September 24, 2003.

regard to this secondary criminal activity said that five mobile phones had been found in his cell the day before his transfer. This no longer appears any great surprise as far as French prisons are concerned, although five does seem rather a lot. What is perhaps more alarming is that his cell had already been thoroughly searched just one week previously...

In April 2004, an individual born in Corsica, strongly suspected of terrorism, was incarcerated. His telephone calls had been under surveillance, and activity was noticed on his line even in the days following his arrival at La Santé prison—he began to call his wife regularly. The police listened attentively and, in addition to information they were able to gather concerning the case in hand, they also obtained enough information to arrest a prison guard who had been paid some € 800 to bring the mobile phone in to him.

At the beginning of March 2007, the case of Boubacar Ba, also nicknamed "El Hadj", "Papa" and "The Old One," came before the 16th Chamber of the Paris Criminal Court. As a recidivist, he faced up to twenty years' imprisonment. Guinean by origin, and sixty years old, he had been convicted twice under other identities. He comes into the scope of this study as the leader of an international cocaine trade, once again run by mobile phone from within the walls of La Santé prison.

In August 2004, Ba was imprisoned for "the export of 2 kg of cocaine" to Belgium. Far from ending the trafficking, his detention gave his business a tremendous boost. For the President of the Court—naïve or willfully ignorant?—this was "the most puzzling paradox that we had to judge in this matter."! Using nothing but his mobile phone, Boubacar Ba had established a complete trade route from South America to Switzerland and back via France. His system was highly developed. Sometimes the drugs would be shipped by container to Cotonou, in Benin, where Ba's family handled the redirect logistics. Most of the time, however, the merchandise would be sent directly from Bogota to Paris in suitcases, which would then be conveyed to Switzerland, from where they would return, full of banknotes.

The bags traveled alone; Colombian accomplices at the airport[22] were responsible for labeling them and loading them aboard. Alerted by a "short message," their Parisian recipients needed only to identify them when the aircraft landed and take them out of the airport. Each suitcase would contain several dozen kilos of high purity cocaine. Between August 2004 and February 2005, nearly 93 kg—$5.2 million worth—was seized, according to customs.

The cocaine's itinerary was well prepared. In Bogota, the suitcases were placed in the hold of the aircraft by Boubacar Ba's contacts, probably the *cartelito "Norte del Valle"* that "held" the airport.

Alerted no later than three days before sending, Ba would mobilize his team, telling the Colombians who their contact in France would be, and to whom photographs and registration numbers of the baggage in question should be sent. When the plane landed at Charles de Gaulle, Paris, a handler took care to extract the bag and pass it on to

[22] Boubacar Ba had links to *Norte del Valle*, the organization with "control" of Bogota airport at the time.

another accomplice in charge of a vehicle authorized to circulate within, and leave, the airport zone.

To reassure the drug traffickers, Boubacar Ba would designate what was termed "human security" from among the members of his network in Colombia. If the drugs were lost, the Colombians were empowered to take their revenge by eliminating this person. This seems to have happened. A suitcase was seized by customs, and in retaliation the Colombians executed their hostage, whose body was discovered a few months later on the outskirts of Bogota. When another consignment was stolen, this time in France, the network meted out correctional measures to the thief, probably torturing him until he returned the drugs and "disappeared" into the wild.

Denounced by one of his own "mules" in February 2004, Boubacar Ba was immediately wire-tapped. Investigators discovered a traffic with multiple ramifications, involving several international "delegates" in Holland, Switzerland, and Benin. Most of his accomplices, identified one after another, were former prisoners who knew Ba in prison.

During his trial, the "Papa" acknowledged having been the boss of several "teams" instructed "to organize the import of large quantities of cocaine from Colombia" He was sentenced to twelve years in prison. In his cell in Meaux, then Val-de-Reuil, he continued his activities after lights-out, making dozens of phone calls to France, the Netherlands and Africa. He even managed to hide the fact that he was languishing behind bars from his contacts.

And in 2008 he would begin all over again, organizing traffic from these same prison cells.

In December 2011, the Paris Criminal Court examined his case for three weeks. The prosecution demanded eighteen years imprisonment, a minimum of two-thirds to be served, to be followed by permanent exclusion from French territory, as a Guinean national. It seems he had little chance of seeing his four wives, his eighteen children and sixty-seven grandchildren ever again.

More recently...

After six months of investigation, the criminal police in Agen, a town in the southwest of France dismantled a cocaine and ecstasy trafficking network being managed from a prison at Eysses.

Seven people were arrested. 1.1 kilograms of cocaine, 5,000 ecstasy pills and 15,500 Euros were seized. The network's boss, born in 1979, had been locked-up for a previous case involving some 5 kg of cocaine. He oversaw the network from his cell where he had a number of mobile phones, which he changed regularly to avoid detection. His brother, born in 1989, was among those arrested.

Finally, there is another symptomatic fact we may consider. In November 9, 2010 it was reported that a search of certain cells at Muret Prison[23] (in the Haute-Garonne

---

[23] Muret detention center, located in the southern suburbs of Toulouse, was commissioned in 1966. It houses some 625 inmates on long sentences, with a total of 634 places. It has 15,000 m^2 of workshops with modern equipment, including CNC machines used in particular in the manufacture of parts for the aerospace and furniture industries.

département) led a prisoner to run, apparently trying to get rid of a package. The package contained € 12,000 in notes and a 3G mobile phone chip. A strip-search of this individual, who is serving a sentence of eighteen years, also found a quantity of hashish. The UFAP and the SPS, the two unions representing prison guards in France, indicated that the money found was part of a "fairly large-scale drug and mobile phone trafficking operation inside the establishment." For other commentators, it was probably linked to the "intensification of traffic, and the re-establishment of gang structures inside the prison walls." It was revealed at the same time that there had been a violent fight between gangs from different buildings just a month previously, after which a number of knife injuries were treated.

The State Prosecutor at Toulouse, clearly playing down all these facts, said that, "it would be a little too soon" to draw the conclusions that were inevitably drawn, stating that he was waiting for the results of the police investigation.

However, the affair has already led to the indictment of three civilian foremen from the workshop where the inmates work.

Already in 2008, a search in the same detention center led to several individuals being taken into police custody, including another civilian foreman and a janitor, allegedly involved in a huge mobile phone and money trafficking operation. Seeking to minimize the affair, the Prosecutor recognized only that a judicial investigation had been open "for some time" and that this was a "long-term" investigation, only recently switched to its active phase." The unions, however, state that "an inordinate amount of money, mobile phones and even pedophile images" were passing around inside the establishment.[24]

All these examples must lead one to wonder just how far things will go inside our prisons if the problem isn't taken seriously.

The proselytizing and recruitment of inmates by terrorist organizations is another reality from which France is not immune. It is a subject of great concern of which people have started to become aware, but which seems to have been dropped almost as soon as discussion started.

The events of January 2015 brutally brought the problem home. We need not go over those details again, but we may look at another example in this regard. Safé Bourada, born in Burgundy in 1970, is a terrorist linked to the Paris attacks of 1995. Sentenced in 1998 to ten years in prison, he was to pass most of his sentence in a new facility built in 1989, in a small town in Normandy, and which housed a thousand inmates considered "non-hazardous."

While serving his time, Bourada managed to convert a dozen of his fellow prisoners to the simplistic version of Islam known as Salafism, convincing them to follow him in what he believed to be a Jihad. Samir, the murderer, Kaïs the rapist, Stéphane the gangster... French or not, Muslims or not, Bourada spoke to them and often converted them. His style was to make simplistic comments on verses of the

[24] *Trafic de téléphones portables et d'argent dans une prison toulousaine*. Europe 1 (radio station), broadcast 4.45 pm, September 11, 2008.

Qur'an, using his basic Arabic. It is well known that radical preachers always schematize their religious teaching under the pretext of returning to the sources; in fact, it is most often an extreme reduction of Islam, far from the tenets of the religion itself.

In prison, Bourada formed a group, *Ansar al-Fath*.[25] Using smuggled mobile phones, he called his former accomplices, those of the 1995 attacks, to try to convince them to follow him, like his cellmates.

Released in 2004, Bourada went to Egypt under the pretext of studying Arabic. He was arrested again in 2005, suspected of terrorist activities with his fellow prisoners of Ansar al-Fath, sending jihadis to fight in Iraq and planning attacks in France, on the model of the London bombings.

According to anti-terrorism agencies, French prisons are fertile ground for Islamists to recruit potential terrorists. Numerous proselytes[26] operate within the French prison system, and more than 10% are converted, from a prison population of 60,000 detainees, including 2,000 classified as "dangerous." Within this population, prisoners accused of terrorist activities appear less active in proselytizing than are common criminals of Muslim origin, although this may be due to the more rigorous supervision to which they are subject.

Today Islam is the largest religion in French prisons. It is therefore perhaps not surprising that Islamist groups form inside, where extremists actively engage in recruiting with the immediate goal of swelling their ranks in Europe and elsewhere.

These Islamist recruiters in French prisons, sometimes dubbed "*les barbus*" (the bearded ones), are often over thirty years of age with a certain level of education, especially in the sciences. They are thus older and better educated than their recruits. They contact other inmates during group activities, circulating copies of the Koran, books and cassettes. They show great devotion and harass their peers into respecting Ramadan and religious days. Very often, they manage to usurp the true Imams, insufficient in number to minister to the whole French prison system. They thus proclaim themselves the only representatives of Islam. Walking around prison with their prayer mats under their arms, even in otherwise prohibited areas, some even take on the role of Muezzin, announcing the hour of prayer and calling the faithful. The prison guards may even call upon these so-called imams to prevent or to calm tense situations, a compromise that serves to strengthen their authority.

In the context of the French prison, radical Islam, Islamism, Salafism, and Tabligh grow and prosper—the ground is fertile for the emergence of new terrorists, a phenomenon illustrated by the recent story of Mohammed Merah (a petty criminal who attacked police and soldiers in Toulouse in 2012 because of French involvement in Afghanistan) and exacerbated by the emergence of the Syrian problem.

Finally, we may examine the administrative side of the equation. On March 10, 2015, it was reported that a guard at Borgo prison had been arrested. She was accused of having brought between twenty-five and fifty mobile phones in to two inmates over

[25] The "Partisans of Victory."

[26] Some 200 individuals, according to sources.

the course of six months. Purchased for between 80 and 100 Euros, the phones were sold at 400 to 500 Euros. Two prisoners were accused of selling them on, inside the prison—Simon G. and Pierre-Antoine P, sentenced in December 2013 to three years for criminal conspiracy. The sister of one of the detainees involved, along with a former inmate, Rudolf G. were also arrested.[27]

Shortly thereafter,[28] a guard at Laon detention center was arrested on suspicion of drug trafficking and theft inside the establishment. He may have had accomplices among the detainees and other colleagues. Two handguns were seized at his home. He had joined the staff at Laon prison in 2011 and held union responsibilities.

The facts reported here are what doctors might call a symptomatology of the threat of prison criminality, that is to say, "that which reveals a condition."

This symptomatology legitimately allows us to consider that prison gangs, or at least real structures, exist in France, as they do in other countries, which we will shortly discuss.

The brutal manner of Rédoine Faïd's escape should perhaps prompt some serious reflection rather than a few jeremiads and the setting up of a psychological support unit here and there. The symptoms indicate a very worrying situation which, as in many other countries, calls for thought and very specific action. Yet despite these and other examples, despite the contacts they have, despite numerous requests, and despite what they know to be happening, the Ministry of Justice and the prison authorities manage to observe total silence on the subject. We are faced, as ever, with the notion of the "French exception" which believes that "nothing happening elsewhere can happen in France."

Madame Taubira, the Minister of Justice (*Garde des Sceaux*), as I revealed at the beginning of this discourse, goes so far as to say that "the Department of Justice being the ministry responsible for the protection of freedoms, must not find itself in a 'confusion of categories' by having the power to prescribe the direct implementation of intelligence-gathering techniques."

These words were spoken at her hearing by the Committee on Legislation of the National Assembly on the bill relating to intelligence gathering, on Tuesday, March 31, 2015.

She went on to say that it is "undesirable, after consideration, to integrate information from prisons with that of the intelligence community," concluding "Integrating prison information with that of the intelligence community would place us at odds with the constitutional obligations of the Department of Justice, namely the constitutional guarantee of the preservation of freedoms" and, heaven forfend, "The Ministry of Justice would end up prescribing intelligence techniques. This is not a service currently exercised by prison staff."

All this is undoubtedly because there is absolutely nothing troubling going on in the French prisons system, and it is definitely not important to know if it is

[27] *Corse Matin*, March 10, 2015

[28] *L'Aisne nouvelle*, March 25, 2015

anyway, nor to share information, much less cross reference it in any attempt to prevent irreparable consequences.

Let us turn to some more examples, non-exhaustive of course, this time from other countries.

B - South Africa, Pioneer in the Field

In South Africa, the threat of prison criminality has existed since the early twentieth century. Gangs are present in all the country's prisons, most notably in a structure called the "Number."[29]

According to the "Jali Commission" of Inquiry,[30] named for its chairman, "the prison administration has lost its ability to exercise control" and in many prisons criminal organizations have "become the law."[31]

The authorities are unable to ensure the safety of prisoners in custody. Beyond the general disorganization in the running of the prison, these gangs are often responsible for violence and homicide. For many years, one punishment handed out by gangs in South African jails to prisoners who stepped out of line was to have them raped by one or several henchmen with AIDS, a ritual known as the "slow puncture."[32] The cause of the slow death being considered "natural," the murder would not be recorded in the statistics for prison violence, even though it was long evident that deaths from this disease within the South African prison system had grown far faster than in the population at large.

This situation could, perhaps, have been avoided. In September 1912,[33] a meeting of prison directors, convened by the Ministry of Justice, adopted a resolution which stated that in order to fight against prison gangs, it was necessary for membership to be a punishable offense in itself. For unknown reasons, these measures were never implemented.

The Number is not a prison gang by origin. Its members are an extension of the "criminal culture" of the outside world, originating in bands of thieves who ravaged the

---

[29] Gangsters call themselves "Numbers" because historically, South African organizations took numbers as identifiers, the highest of which may not exceed 28. When they have a name, it is incidental.

[30] Commission of Inquiry into prisons chaired by Judge Thabani Jali: Commission of Inquiry into Alleged Incidents of Corruption, Maladministration, Violence or Intimidation in the Department of Correctional Services Appointed by Order of the President of the Republic of South Africa in Terms of Proclamation No. 135 of 2001, as Amended. South Africa Prisons Ministry, November 2006.

[31] According to Dr. Willem Schurink, testifying before the Jali Commission. *Cape Argus*, February 19, 2003.

[32] According to the Director of prison inspections, Gideon Morris, testifying before the Jali Commission (Reuters, 22 November 2002). See also: Maclennan, B., "Slow puncture; death sentence for Prisoners," November 20, 2002 (www.iol.co.za).

[33] State Archives, Department of Justice, Vol 144, No. 1 issue: 31,778,112, quoted in Van Onselen, C., *Regiment of the Hills*, unpublished. See Haysom, Nicholas. *Towards an understanding of Prison Gangs*. Republic of South Africa: University of Cape Town Institute of Criminology, 1981, 15.

mining towns of the Transvaal. Legend and reality, mythology, rituals and symbols[34] are intertwined in its history, although opinions differ on how its "culture" truly developed.

All opinions agree, however, on the role of an individual known as Nongoloza,[35] and the oral tradition relates that the gang's origins date back to a group of bandits known as the Ninevites, (a name taken from the inhabitants of Nineveh, in Mesopotamia, "heathen idolaters, denying God" according to the Bible).[36] These bandits left their native lands for Johannesburg, where they scourged a growing city, stealing from mine owners and their employees. Other gangs, including the "26s," claim that everything started before even that, in around 1830, when a certain Paul Mo Basa, a notorious robber was later joined by two rival gangs, those of Kilikijane and Nongoloza.

According to this version of the legend, Kilikijane and Nongoloza each had his own gang. Nongoloza operated at night while Kilikijane ruled the day. Organizing his members according to a military hierarchy, Nongoloza created the largest and most notorious gang in Southern Africa. Certain members claim that its goals had become political and economic, as they only stole from the white oppressor. In reality, black people were just as often his victims, especially in the immigrant townships that were springing up everywhere.

The Ninevites thus became a formidable criminal organization, bringing the art of fraud, theft and robbery to a peak. Many of them were thrown in prison, Nongoloza among them. He made it his mission to maintain the loyalty of the Ninevites incarcerated in prisons of the Witwatersrand and in other cities of the Transvaal.

While stories of the origins of the Number call upon both myth and reality, their criminal activity in South African prisons is very real indeed. The organizations posing the greatest problem for the prison administration system are three in number, all highly organized. Because Nongoloza was known for having sexual relations with other men—something the Kilikijane gang would not tolerate—the Ninevites split into two gangs, the 27s and the 28s. In contrast to these, the 26s were formed in prison.

The 28s. This is the most direct descendant of the Ninevites and is the largest of the Number gangs. Its main goals are based on food, wyfies[37]—the "boy-wives" —and fighting against abuses of power by the prison administration. Like the other Number gangs, the 28s claim that membership is voluntary and that they do not recruit members already owned by other gangs. While the youngest members earn their colors as wyfies, the eldest are the soldiers. The leaders are entitled to their own wyfies chosen from among the new arrivals, while other members are free to have sex with young recruits.

---

[34] The arcane and finely observed military and judicial hierarchies of the 28s and the 27s are precisely those invented by Nongoloza and described in the life testimony he dictated to a prison warder in 1912. For Nongoloza's life testimony. Department of Justice, Annual Report for the Year 1912, 237–240.

[35] His real name was Mzuzephi Mathebula. See Haysom, *Towards an Understanding of Prison Gangs*.

[36] Ninevites, the inhabitants of Biblical Nineveh (a city in Mesopotamia, today Mosul, Iraq). Bible books Nahum and especially Jonas recount opposition between Ninevites, idolaters and pagans, and the chosen people of Israel, who worshipped Jehovah.

[37] Boy-wife, often the youngest prisoners, who serve as "women."

Promotion is earned through knowledge of the gang's rules and acts of bravery.

The 27s: Legend has it that the gang was created by seven dissidents from the Nongoloza gang, horrified by the practice of taking wyfies. This gang was once extensive, but scarcely exists in most prisons today.[38] Its objective is to maintain peace between the Number gangs and make rules establishing relationships between them. It "renders justice by revenge and sheds blood where blood has been shed."

The 26s: Six inmates saved Kilikijane, detained in solitary confinement in Point Prison (Durban), by passing him bread and salt through a crack in the door. Thus was created the third "camp"[39] of prisoners, formed under the condition set by Nongoloza, that their name (number) would be lower than the others and that no fourth "camp" would ever be formed.[40]

Since its formation, the emblem of the 26s has been the Kroon,[41] believed to bring wealth.

Its members live in "luxury" obtained by theft[42] of property, money and dagga[43] from other inmates and by bringing products of value into the prison. It is forbidden for them to speak with representatives of the prison administration without permission, except to make a complaint or demand. Members can never resign, and when they "retire", they can never join another gang. Sexual relationships between members of the gang are prohibited.

Other smaller and more localized gangs exist alongside the Number gangs, who are generally enemies. This is especially the case of the Big 5 gang,[44] the Airforce,[45] the Desperados[46] and other minor gangs.[47]

---

[38] Except in Cape Province.

[39] Synonym for gang.

[40] Steinberg, Jonny. *Nongoloza's Children: Western Cape Prison Gangs during and after Apartheid.* Monograph written for the Centre for the Study of Violence and Reconciliation, July 2004, 10.

[41] Crown, a coin in the mythology of the Numbers. Used as a gambling chip.

[42] "Collect your Blood," *The Witness*, February 4, 2005, article in which it is suggested that "thieving" should be the motto of the 26s.

[43] Locally produced cannabis.

[44] Created in the 1950s, their main objective was to aid escapes but when their leader, Masondo, was killed in an escape attempt, the gang decided to work with members of the Correctional Services. Members of this gang do not observe solidarity, which may be regarded as the cornerstone of the prison code. The Big 5s are also reputed to wear rubber boots called ganders with which enable them to deliver violent blows to their adversaries.

[45] The main objective of this gang is to escape from prison. Members of this gang hold that, unlike some of the other gangs, membership is voluntary. Promotion within the gang depends on the number of escapes or escape attempts made. One of their modus operandi is to start a fight between two gangs to distract the prison guards. Homosexual relationships are prohibited. Communication with Correctional Services members is restricted to complaints or requests, as they fear that discussion may lead to exposure of gang secrets. See *Collect your Blood.*

[46] Recent, unusual and limited to the Cape, almost exclusively composed of colored prisoners. See "Manual for visitors to independent prisons." (Section 85-1 Correctional Services Act 111 of 1998, 1998), Office of the Judge-Inspector, Judicial Inspectorate of Prisons in South Africa.

[47] Such as the Forty Thieves, Spy 13, Fast Eleven, Flick Styles, Boek 30's, Shy Boys, Fast Twelve, Black Power etc. Haysom, *Towards an Understanding of Prison Gangs.*

C - USA: An Alternative Form of Organized Crime

After ten years of proceedings, a trial began on April 6, 2015 in Denver, Colorado, placing some of America's most notorious gangsters on the stand.[48]

The boss of the Mexican Mafia in the Administrative Maximum Facility (ADX), Florence, Texas,[49] Silvestre "Chikali" Mayorqui-Rivera, stands accused of having fatally beaten Manuel "Tati" Torrez, a member of the Mexican Mafia Hard Core, transferred from California. The case dates back to April 21, 2005 and the events occurred during an exercise period in the prison yard.

Chikali faces life imprisonment for first degree murder. His accomplice Richard "Chuco" Santiago, also serving a life sentence for a similar crime, risks the death penalty. The accused are being tried separately.

Chikali and Torrez should never have been in the yard at the same time without guards in the immediate vicinity. The response teams were slow to arrive, after having mobilized to the wrong area. By the time of their arrival Torrez was dead. It was learned that the whole scenario was a trap which backfired against Torrez—a premeditated and revealing act, which should not have been allowed to happen in one of the most closely supervised American prisons.

What Americans call "prison gangs" are structured criminal networks whose activities extend around the federal prison structure and across state boundaries. The gangs also operate in the outside world, via members released from prison. They usually return to their home communities and reconnect with the gang to which they belonged. They act as representatives of the prison gangs and recruit members of street gangs to carry out criminal acts on their behalf.

Prison gangs control, among other things, the distribution of drugs within prisons. They now also have a dominant influence over their distribution in the street in certain areas, especially through the links they maintain with the Mexican cartels, which ensure a continuous supply.

Of the five national-level prison gangs, two have members or partners in at least two foreign countries. Prison gangs are well organized and governed by a code and established rules, rigorously applied by the gang leaders.

Regional prison gangs, confined to the prison systems of no more than one or two states, represent a more modest, although growing threat, as ever more links with drug suppliers are forged. The largest "regional" prison gang operates in Texas.

Local or state gangs, especially those located along the border between the United States and Mexico, have long had links with Mexican cartels, and can be among the most dangerous. On April 11, 2014, members and associates of the Texas Mexican Mafia, including one "general," were sentenced to long prison terms for their roles in drug trafficking and racketeering. At Del Rio, Javier Guerrero, 24, was sentenced to three consecutive life sentences "with a supplement of 210 months" for racketeering in prison and attacking a guard. Meanwhile, in San Antonio, "general" Robert "Lil Bit"

[48] *Denver Post*, April 6, 2015.

[49] United States Penitentiary, Administrative Maximum Facility (ADX)

Carreno was sentenced to 300 months in prison, along with eight other people, for selling 48 kg of heroin, bringing in revenue of $750,000 for the gang between December 2009 and July 2011. He also ripped the nose off a guard as he awaited another verdict. The conviction of prisoners is commonplace.

On June 9, 2002, Mariano "Chuy" Martinez, Los Angeles boss of the Mexican Mafia,[50] the *Eme*,[51] the most formidable prison gang in the United States, was sentenced to life imprisonment. In order to establish his authority, he ordered three murders and sponsored a dozen others from his cell.

On May 22, 2000, Gustavio Gino Colon,[52] one of the "brains" of the Latin Kings,[53] was also sentenced to life imprisonment while incarcerated. What for? As in the case at Saint-Quentin-Fallavier, he ran a drug trafficking ring by mobile phone from the high security Menard prison in Illinois,[54] where he was already serving a heavy sentence.[55] This leader, who until then enjoyed a privileged status, to the extent that he even had a key to his "room" and had meals served to him by his henchmen,[56] ran a network covering the whole of Illinois, managing his "business" and also ordering executions outside the prison walls.[57]

Does this easy permeability between prisons and the outside world represent any kind of paradox? The answer is no, as we shall see later. In any case, the domination is real. At the end of September 1993, the Mexican Mafia imposed a "truce" on all Hispanic gangs in Los Angeles, outlawing the practice of drive-by shooting[58] as "detrimental to business."[59] To the surprise of observers,[60] the order[61] was scrupulously respected.

---

[50] Formed in 1956 to 1957 in a California prison, the Deuel Vocational Institute (DVI) in Tracy. This prison gang is also known as the Gang of Gangs. Outside California, the Mexican Mafia is present in Arizona, Colorado, Florida, Hawaii, Illinois, Kansas, Nevada, New Mexico, Oregon, Texas, Utah, Washington, Wisconsin, and Mexico. Nonetheless, only some 300 members and around 900 associates are suspected. The National Gang Threat assessment, 2009, considers that it has authority over between 50,000 and 75,000 Sureños gang members.

[51] The letter "M" in Spanish, 13th letter of the alphabet. The number "13" is a reference to the Gangs of Southern California and, by extension, all those standing behind the *Eme*.

[52] Also called "Lord" Gino.

[53] Or the "Almighty Latin King Nation," a gang from Chicago, which first appeared in the 1940s and is among the largest in the United States.

[54] Some of his calls were recorded. *Chicago Tribune*, September 5, 1999.

[55] Chester, Illinois, United States.

[56] Colon, still wearing the "uniform" of his gang, enjoyed great freedom of movement and had the key to his "room" where his meals were served to him by his cronies. Steve Macko, Emergency Response and Research Institute (ERRI), Special Report, May 12, 1997.

[57] Including that of a guard at Stateville Correctionnal Center (near Joliet, Illinois), not proven, in 1989. See below.

[58] An operation in which other Gangsters are shot at from a moving car, often causing serious "collateral damage" and therefore an increased police activity in the area concerned.

[59] Lopez, Robert J. and Jesse Katz "Mexican Mafia Tells Gangs to Halt Drive-Bys." *LA Times*, September 26, 1993.

[60] It so happened that the author was in Los Angeles at that time and conversations he had with police revealed that they were extremely doubtful that this decision by the Eme could have any effect in the street.

[61] Here is the text of the handwritten manifesto of the Mexican Mafia: "To all, young and old, members

Acquiescence? Intimidation?[62] In the neighborhoods concerned, drive-by shootings are rare to this day.[63]

This control of the street can take other forms. On January 16, 2004, the San Diego (California) Sheriff's office issued a security bulletin to its personnel, according to which imprisoned high-ranking members of the Eme had ordered members of the Mesa and Center Street gangs to attack police officers and members of the Sheriff's office, wherever they came into contact with them and whenever they were armed. Any Eme gang member not obeying was to be "taken care of."

On October 15, 2004, the email network of an association of American police officers distributed "serious" vigilance information to its members. Imprisoned leaders of the Aryan Brotherhood, an extensive prison gang, had ordered, from their cells, the execution of five California police officers or members of their families, to be selected at random, in retaliation for an operation carried out against the gang a few weeks previously. This kind of extraordinary threat is taken seriously, and is far from isolated. Prison crime can take other forms. Take for example what is now called "Prislam" in the United States. A number of proselytizing groups have appeared, often successfully converting prisoners from all backgrounds, and belonging to all types of communities. One may consider that, initially, Islam was used in prisons by certain people as a means of obtaining special facilities, this being said with all respect due to that religion. It would seem that non-Muslim prisoners are able to exploit the practice of Islam, with its daily congregational prayers and dedicated facilities, to thwart the surveillance of the guards for criminal purposes. This is undoubtedly not true everywhere, but it certainly appears in the reflections of Kody "Monster" Scott.

In his book, "Monster"[64] Kody Scott, an Original Gangster of the Eight Tray Crips of Los Angeles, says that when he was placed in the Youth Training School (a prison for young offenders located in Chino) in 1983, Islam was not widespread. But when it came to preparing an "operation" with the twenty-three other prisoners in his gang, the only place they could meet without drawing the attention of guards was the room reserved for the Muslim faith.[65] Monster Kody assiduously followed the devotions and ended up converting to Islam, taking the name Sanyika Shakur. He is now a member of the New African Movement, and is engaged in political activism.

---

of Latino Street Gangs, the power inside the walls clearly states that all acts of violence will now be considered a lack of respect for the *Eme* and all those enforcing peace in your neighborhoods. If you choose not to respect the truce you will pay with your life. If you have a problem with a rival, you must fix it with him. We have to respect each other, otherwise we will never be united or represent a true power in our cities. I- Respect the Eme. II- Respect the elders. III- Respect the truce."

[62] *Los Angeles Times*, October 1, 1993.

[63] Perhaps also because the Eme truce directive allowed walk-up shootings to continue *Gang Beat*, 12, 4, (Summer 2001).

[64] Shakur, Sanyika (alias Kody Scott). *Monster, the autobiography of an L.A. gang member*. New York: Atlantic Monthly Press, 1993.

[65] Shakur. *Monster*, 209.

By August 2005, California Federal Attorney Debra Yang indicted Kevin Lamar James,[66] a member of the Crips, sentenced to ten years in prison for armed robbery and locked up since 1996 in Folsom, things were somewhat different. James was the founder, in 1997, and leader of an Islamist prison gang, the *Jam'iyyat Ul-Islam is Saheeh* (JIS),[67] which the FBI suspected of planning attacks in the south of the state.[68] For the deputy director of public relations, John Miller, "this terrorist organization was the closest to succeeding operationally since 9/11."[69] The members of this gang mainly converted to Islam in prison—a good example being that of Jose Padilla,[70] the man behind the "dirty bomb" of 2002. James pleaded guilty in December 2007 and has since admitted that the attacks had been prepared by JIS and financed by money from armed attacks against official buildings and Jewish interests in southern California.

The Muslim prison population is around 20%, and most are African-Americans converted to Islam in prison, where gangs represent a greater danger than terrorism. Nonetheless, in 2006, a report by Homeland Security warned that every "radicalized" prisoner is a potential recruit for terrorism, and called for action to be taken before an attack occurs.

D - Latin America

1 - Brazil: Hybridization

In Brazil, the *Primeiro Comando da Capital* (PCC)[71] reigns supreme over prison life, above all in the São Paulo region.[72] This organization was created by eight prisoners[73] after a football match on August 31, 1993 in the Taubaté high-security prison, São

---

[66] As well as Levar Haney Washington, Gregory Vernon Patterson and Hammad Riaz Samana, of Pakistani origin.

[67] Association for authentic Islam.

[68] Testimony of Donald Van Duyn, Deputy Director of Counterterrorism, FBI, appearing before the Senate (http://www.fbi.gov/ congress/congress06/vanduyn091906.htm); testimony of William Bratton, Chief of Police of Los Angeles in the House of Representatives (http://www.investigativeproject.org/documents/testimony/276.pdf) Harris, Robert. "Kevin James and the JIS conspicacy." *Frontline*, October 10, 2006.

[69] www.historycommons.org/entity.jsp?entity=jam_iyyat_ul_islam_is_saheeh_1

[70] Or Abdullah al Muhajir or Muhajir Abdullah, a member of the Maniac Latin Disciples gang of Chicago, converted to Islam in prison.

[71] The capital of the State of São Paulo, São Paulo. The PCC was later known as the "Party of crime" and also 15.3.3 (order of the letters in the Brazilian Portuguese alphabet).

[72] This is not the only prison organization in Brazil, there are also the "CDL," the "Satanic Cult," the "Dragons," and especially the *Comando Vermelho* (Red Commando), one of the principal Rio gangs, founded in jail between 1969 and 1975. In August 2008, one of its leaders, Fernando Da Costa, aka "Beira-Mar", 40, was sentenced by a court in Rio to six years in prison for "association with criminals for drug trafficking purposes." Sentenced with him were several of his accomplices, also members of the Comando Vermelho. Beira-Mar is a major drug godfather in Rio. Sentenced in 2005 to 18 years in prison, he continued to head the network from his cell. *Ultima Instancia*, August 15, 2008

[73] Misael Misa Aparecido da Silva, Wander Eduardo Cara Gorda Ferreira, Antonio Carlos Roberto da

Paulo (known as Piranhão).[74] The political motivation was evident—the PCC was formed to "fight oppression in the prison system of São Paulo" and "avenge the deaths of 111 prisoners, victims of the repression of October 2, 1992" at Carandiru.[75] The Chinese *taijitu* symbol, representing the Yin and Yang, was chosen as their emblem, "a way to balance good and evil with wisdom" according to the founders of the PCC.

In February 2001, Carlos Ambrósio Idemir Sombra became the most prominent leader of the organization, which referred to itself as "the Syndicate" at the time. The gang was initially quite unobtrusive, but then Sombra used a mobile phone to organize and coordinate one of the largest prison revolts in history. 27,000 inmates simultaneously took control of twenty-nine prisons and kept 14,000 people[76] hostage for twenty-seven hours. Although sixteen detainees were killed, it was ample demonstration to the country's authorities of the power of the PCC to mobilize. Five months later, Sombra, also known as "Father" was beaten to death at a Piranhão by five members of a more highly criminalized faction of the PCC in search of power. This was duly seized by Césinha and Geleião, founders of the PCC and originators of an alliance with the *Comando Vermelho*, one of the major criminal organizations in Rio de Janeiro.

From the maximum security facility at Bangu, in which they were both incarcerated, the two leaders organized attacks against public buildings and used terrorist methods to intimidate the prison authorities. Considered too violent, they were removed from power in November 2002.

The organization was then taken over by Marcos "Marcola" Herbas Camacho, also known as the "Playboy."[77] He immediately put a bounty on the heads of his predecessors for betrayal to the authorities and for founding a dissident group, the *Terceiro Comando da Capital* or TCC.

Marcola, like the others, took a hard line against officials of the authorities, and the PCC was suspected of killing two judges in 2003,[78] including Antônio José Machado Diaz,[79] director of the Penitentiary Readaptation Center (CRP),[80] the most secure prison in the country. For sponsoring this crime, Marcola was sentenced to twenty-nine years in prison. The PCC also announced among its objectives, its intention to generate and use the uprisings in prisons to "demoralize the government" and "destroy the CRP." The leaders of the PCC give their orders using mobile phones brought into

---

Paixão, Isaías Esquisito Moreira do Nascimento, Ademar Dafé dos Santos, Antônio Bicho Feio Carlos dos Santos, César Césinha Augusto Roris da Silva and José Geleião Màricio Felício

[74] The "Great Piranha."

[75] The military police stormed the detention center and killed all the prisoners of Pavilion No. 9.

[76] Guards and visitors.

[77] Sentenced to 44 years in prison for drug trafficking and attacks using firearms, he has been inside since 1999. His eclectic tastes are demonstrated by the literature found in his cell: The Art of War by Sun Tzu, The Prince by Machiavelli and biographies of Che Guevara.

[78] Two judges specialized in the fight against organized crime were murdered in the month of March 2003 in Brazil. The PCC was the prime suspect. *Financial Times*, March 23, 2003.

[79] Marcola was sentenced to 29 years in prison for ordering the murder of Judge Antônio José Machado Diaz in São Paulo in March 2003. AP November 13, 2009.

[80] In the district of Presidente Bernardes, São Paulo, Brazil.

the prisons by henchmen or sympathizers, either obeying orders or willing to render services for money. Not only phones make their way into prisons, but also drugs, weapons, prostitutes and food. Since its show of force, the PCC has been politicizing its proclamations and is implicated in the assassination of judges and the funding of escapes.[81] The authorities appear to be overwhelmed.

On April 22, 2004 another rebellion in the Brazilian prison of Porto Velho came to an end. Competition between two rival gangs led to five days of violence, the deaths of nine people and 170 taken hostage. A thousand inmates controlled all the buildings. In addition, three tunnels were discovered and destroyed: this indicated the preparation of a mass escape, probably the origin of the feud between the prison gangs.[82]

In June 2005, a riot at the CRP ended with the deaths of five prisoners—undoubtedly traitors to the PCC, whose heads were displayed on spikes on the roof. In December of the same year, twelve different operations targeted buses and police. The final count was 19 dead and 20 wounded.

In May 2006, as ever from their cells using mobile phones, the leaders of the PCC, under the direction of Marcola, directly challenged the São Paulo authorities in response to their plan[83] to destroy the PCC by splitting its leaders up and getting rid of them. Three hundred separate attacks were executed simultaneously against public buildings and police stations, public transportation and banks. Seventy prisons suffered riots. For several days, the region experienced unprecedented pressure in a climate of near civil war. 43 policemen and 91 attackers were killed (170 people in total according to some sources); sixty buses were burned.

Since these events, the PCC has been monitored more closely, especially in the prisons holding its most important leaders. As a result of this pressure and losses incurred, the PCC later had difficulty meeting its expenses. Wire taps made in September 2006 revealed difficulties providing the "social services" usually available to the families of its imprisoned or dead members, especially as recruiting to rebuild its numbers required it to halve the "dues" levied on its members.[84] The PCC has also been forced to decentralize parts of its command structure to compensate for the loss of some leaders and the more stringent containment measures imposed on others.

More recently, it seems that the PCC has turned to other ambitions—it is seeking no less than representation at the Brazilian parliament. Police reportedly intercepted a conversation between Daniel Vinicius "El Ciego" Canonico, a Marcola spokesman and a lawyer for the organization.[85] The strategy of the PCC appears to be the funding of

---

[81] In São Paulo, the number of escapes rose from 552 in 1999 to 1023 in 2000. However, they were not always successful: On November 8, 2003, more than 80 prisoners who tried to escape through tunnels in São Paulo were met by the police as they came out. A number of others died of suffocation in the tunnel.

[82] AP, April 22, 2004.

[83] Presented at a confidential meeting and immediately communicated to a lawyer for the PCC by a sympathizer.

[84] *See below.*

[85] *El Pais*, April 3, 2008.

certain election campaigns and influencing votes in at least ten states of the country, particularly through the families of imprisoned members and their "associates" outside. In the words of this lawyer, the PCC is sufficiently powerful and influential to win parliamentary representation, and he goes so far as to compare the gang to the IRA and Sinn Fein.

In February 2014 it was reported, according to police intelligence, that the PCC was planning to have Marcola sprung from jail. Imprisoned in Presidente Venceslau prison, Marcola and three other leaders of the CPC (Barbara Claudio da Silva; Celio Marcelo da Silva, known as "Bin Laden" and Luiz Eduardo Marcondes Machado, known as "De La Bela Vista") planned an escape by air. A commando helicopter was to arrive in the colors of the Military Police, to take away the four men in an armored pod. Another helicopter, equipped with a machine gun, was to ensure the protection of the first aircraft. A small plane was waiting to take the bosses to Paraguay. The authorities initially considered transferring those involved in the plan to a prison with a strict disciplinary regime, but the PCC is said to have threatened to disrupt the inauguration of the World Cup in San Paulo on June 12, 2014. Some observers, however, think that this affair may have been exaggerated at a time when elections were about to take place.

Since then, according to the Brazilian intelligence services, the PCC has made a number of agreements with Hezbollah,[86] which is very active in the "tri-border area" between Argentina, Brazil and Paraguay. In exchange for protection of their members imprisoned in Brazil, Hezbollah facilitates the trafficking of arms and explosives to the PCC. This agreement was concluded in 2006, notably through a travel agent called Farouk Abdul Hay Omairi, regarded as the coordinator of Hezbollah in Brazil. He was sentenced in 2007 to 12 years in prison for drug trafficking. He has been out on parole since 2012.

2 - Venezuela: Extreme Violence

September 17, 2013 saw a battle between gangs which left sixteen people dead in the Venezuelan prison of Maracaibo, known as "La Sabaneta." This was a conflict between *pranes*[87] for control of the different prison wings. The battle began when Edwin "El Mocho" Soto, head of the gang *El Tren del Norte*, and thirty of his men knocked down a wall to invade the territory of another gang.

Equipped with bulletproof vests, firearms, grenades and Molotov cocktails, Soto's men forced their rivals to surrender then slaughtered them all. *Pran* Ricardo Moreno had his heart cut from his chest, his brother Engelbert Moreno, another *pran*, was also killed, while a third brother, Ronald Moreno had his eyes gouged out. Engelbert Anez, another prisoner, was castrated and had his ears cut off. A third *pran*, Jobel Valenciano was completely dismembered. Photos of the massacre were then

[86] *O Globo*, November 9, 2014.

[87] *Pran*, pl. *pranes*: prison criminal gang leader.

circulated on social networks. Since then, "El Mocho" Soto has been *El Gran Pran de Maracaibo*. By January 2013, battles between gangs had caused the deaths of sixty-one inmates.

3 - Honduras, El Salvador: Barbaric Competition

A "ticking time bomb" is how the El Porvenir prison, was described by José Edgardo Coca, president of the Association of Prisoners at this establishment. This was his analysis when eighty members of the Mara 18[88] were transferred to the prison in February 2003; "La Mara[89] is unmanageable" he declared, and indeed Mario Roberto Cerrato, leader of the Mara managed to injure him using a pistol[90] on April 5th. This event caused running battles between the two gangs, which were then suppressed with extreme violence by the authorities—sixty-eight dead in total, including sixty-one members of the Mara. The Deputy Minister of State Security, Armando Calidonio was to declare "it is incredible that nothing happened the other 364 days of the year."[91]

Since then, twenty policemen and soldiers have been sentenced to between three and thirty years[92] for the bloody suppression of the El Porvenir prison battle. "The involvement of police and army was shown to be part of a policy of extermination of young people involved with the Maras," said the judge of the court of La Ceiba, which retained charges of murder, attempted murder and violation of the duties of a public official. The Human Rights Court prosecution revealed in November 2004 that the police had supplied weapons to the prisoners who had led the mutiny. Similar accusations have been made in other countries.

Tensions and violence also flared in El Salvador where the Mara 18 and MS 13 pursue their street war in prison, often in the most barbaric way. This was the case in the maximum security prison of Apanteos, near the city of Santa Ana. According to the Prosecutor for Human Rights, Beatrice Alamanni, "it was a bloody massacre—heads and feet could be seen under the rubble inside the cells." Twenty-one people were killed, often decapitated or disemboweled with makeshift weapons. Photographs corroborate these claims.

---

[88] A Central American offshoot of the 18th Street gang. Started in Los Angeles in the mid-1960s, it is one of the most powerful gangs in the US with around 50,000 members and associates. Hispanic in origin, it was the first gang to accept members from all backgrounds.

[89] "The Gangs of Central America are called *Maras*, a term inspired a species of highly aggressive ants [marabuntas], which attack in swarms." *Crackdown on Gangs Brings Mexico Violence*, AP, December 10, 2003.

[90] Which was never found.

[91] *New York Times*, May 20, 2003.

[92] In June 2008.

E - Europe

1 - Italy

Contrary to the reputation the mafia once had of abandoning its criminal activities and avoiding attention while in prison, the Italian police have shown that mafia bosses pursue their activities from inside, using their wives, parents, friends and subordinates to transmit instructions through signs, gestures or messages,[93] allowing their organization to function. This permeability is well known, but more structured organizational forms exist in Italian prisons too.

La *Nuova Camorra Organizzata* (NCO), the most dangerous camorra federation[94] between 1970 and 1980, was created within the prison system by Raffaele Cutolo, an individual who has spent most of his life in prison.[95] Cutolo built his organization by helping young men, mostly inexperienced and poor, to survive in prison. He then strengthened it by setting up a system of financial aid to prisoners and their families, based on "taxation" of the criminal activity of released affiliates.

In parallel, Cutolo led the *Nuova Camorra Organizzata* down an avenue of ultra-violence, giving it a near monopoly in a large number of prisons, which it ruled through intimidation and murder. It was a classical system of "carrot and stick" but also of corruption, given that Cutolo had the power to select the cells and jails his members would be sent to, in order to better develop his power structure. He himself enjoyed virtually free use of the prison director's office telephone. Ultimately it was the arrogance and paranoia of Cutolo himself, particularly his irrational use of murder, even within the ranks of his own organization, along with the onslaught of the *Nuova Famiglia*[96] and the police, which led the NCO to ruin.

2 - UK

Every year thousands of detainees are beaten, bullied or intimidated by increasingly numerous and violent gangs that develop as the prison population grows. Gangs engage in all sorts of illegal activities—drug trafficking, gambling, assault and murder. Some have become so powerful that they bring in revenues of hundreds of pounds a week to their members, set aside for release or used to improve life inside the prison. The prison administration has been overwhelmed by the arrival of the drug and gang culture that has penetrated its institutions.

---

[93] Called *pizzinis* like those found in large numbers in the cache of Bernardo Provenzano when he was arrested in 2006.

[94] *Camorra*: a criminal organization originally from Naples (Italy) and Campania. Raufer, X. *La Camorra, une mafia urbaine*. Paris: La Table Ronde, 2005.

[95] Behan, Tom. "*See Naples and die.*" *The Camorra and organized crime*. London, New York: I.B. Tauris Books, 2002.

[96] A rival federation which, at that time, united all the most important families of the Camorra.

In Liverpool,[97] one of the largest prisons in England (1400 inmates), drugs and brutality are so commonplace that some prisoners prefer never to leave their cells. Detainees interviewed described drugs as either "easy" or "very easy" to obtain, and 30% of drug tests have been shown to be positive, an even higher rate than in other prisons. During the summer of 2004, seventy-three assaults involving the use of weapons were recorded against other inmates. Often prisoners on cleaning duties will disconnect cell alarms and surveillance cameras, preventing guards from watching certain places within the prison. Intimidation and threats are commonplace and extend out to the families[98] of other inmates.

In April 2015, one former manager in the British Prison Service, Peter Hiett,[99] revealed a number of serious cases of extreme failure that he had witnessed during his career. He was forced to retire in January 2014 after attempting to denounce some particularly shocking practices. His revelations concerning events in the juvenile prison in Feltham, in the suburbs west of London, are terrifying and alarming. No fewer than forty-eight different gangs continue their territorial disputes within the walls of this facility; some manage to control entire wings, to the extent that staff do not dare to enter. Peter Hiett claimed that guards organize fights between inmates in rooms specially equipped to ensure that injuries are not too serious; he was once required to report a female guard for having sex with a teenager, jailed for murder, in his cell.[100] His closing remark was to the effect that all statistics concerning the establishment were systematically revised downwards. Elsewhere he denounced the gang microculture within the facility: "We are transforming our youth into far worse criminals than they were ever going to be when they arrived. They are incarcerated for minor offenses and are transformed into drug traffickers"

The use of mobile phones (thrown over the perimeter wall and picked up by prisoners allowed to work near the wall under instructions from the gangs) has allowed the creation of extensive drugs networks inside. The criminal underworld of Liverpool is highly organized, and wouldn't let a little matter like being in prison put a stop to its business.

The authorities of Shotts prison in Scotland placed one detainee, James McDonald, 35, in solitary confinement, accused of leading a drug and weapons trafficking network from his cell. McDonald was sentenced in May 2008 to life imprisonment, with a minimum tariff of 35 years. A similar sentence was handed down to his accomplice Raymond Anderson, 47, for a murder and two attempted

---

[97] Travis, Allan, and Eric Allison. "Prison Overwhelmed by Gang Culture." Section on a report made by Chief Inspector of Prisons, Anne Owers. *The Guardian*, January 18, 2005.
[98] Thompson, Tony. "Gangs Bring Terror and Death to Jails." Section on Cathy James, governor of Walton prison. *The Observer*, January 23, 2005.
[99] *Daily Mirror*, April 11, 2015.
[100] Emma Beard sent love letters and intimate photographs to Danny McLean, 18, sentenced to 15 years in prison for stabbing Shakilus Townsend, 16, in 2009. She was sentenced to 12 months in prison. Married Woman Prison Officer who had Sex with Teenage 'Honey Trap Killer' in his Cell is Jailed for 12 Months. *Daily Mail*, December 7, 2010.

murders. Anderson was moved to another prison after boasting that "more people work for me than the chief warden" at Shotts.[101]

The same situation prevails around the country. Two main types of prison gangs responsible for violence have been identified. First are those who import ongoing street conflicts between gangs for control of territory into the prison. The other type is those who feed racial tensions, exacerbated by the emergence of white supremacists as in the United States.[102] Many murders are attributable to such racial conflicts. Other conflicts originate entirely in prison, the classic example being a "lack of respect" toward gang leaders.

The situation has improved somewhat, with opportunities for education and work available to inmates. Nevertheless some forty percent of them prefer to remain idle. It is hoped that the measures taken will help in the fight against the proliferation of gangs and drug trafficking in prison[103] but questions remain while it is easier for an inmate to sell drugs than to work or learn.[104]

Some prisons are more sensitive than others, depending on their specialty. As such, Full Sutton prison is where the most important drug lords, terrorists and gangsters with extensive resources on the outside are sent (a number have been transferred from Whitemoor since the discovery of a large stash of mobile phones in that prison). Here the exercise areas have been covered with mesh to prevent helicopter escapes, at least two of which were foiled in 2005.[105] Conversely, Wakefield is reserved for serious sex offenders with no significant financial means and whom nobody wants to help.

Islamist Fundamentalism and Prison

In 2006, Muslims in UK prisons numbered more than 8,000—6% of British nationality— representing 11% of the prison population; 25% were serving sentences for drug trafficking. Since then, the number of Muslim prisoners has skyrocketed, in part because of terrorism, but mostly because of the large number of criminal offenses committed by illegal immigrants and young British Muslims.

Taking advantage of the facilities granted to religious groups in prison, some form their gangs in these places, avoiding the attention of prison management, and gradually taking control of the prison. Muslim inmates at the high security Whitemoor

---

[101] *Daily Record*, November 30, 2009.

[102] Thompson, Tony. *Gangs Brings Terror And Death To Jails*. Section on Kimmett Edgar, Director of Studies of the Prison Reform Trust. *The Observer*, January 23, 2005.

[103] Travis, Allan, and Eric Allison. "Prison Overwhelmed by Gang Culture." Section on Phil Wheatley, Director General of the Prison Service. The Guardian, January 18, 2005.

[104] Travis, Allan, and Eric Allison. "Prison Overwhelmed by Gang Culture." Section on Juliet Lyon, Prison Reform Trust. *The Guardian*, January 18, 2005.

[105] O'Hara, Kate. Article on a report by Deputy Director of the Prison Service, Peter Atherton. *The Yorkshire Post*, April 13, 2005.

[106] Including Saajid Badat, the accomplice of Richard Reid, the shoe bomber.

prison,[106] accounting for a third of the 500 prisoners, created a climate of fear and insecurity both for guards and other detainees[107] to the extent that upon arrival, non-Muslim prisoners were warned by the management of the existence of these gangs, and of the growing tensions between the guards and black and ethnic minorities.[108] The guards are reluctant to suppress offensive behavior by the minorities for fear of being accused of politically incorrect attitudes, or being sanctioned for racism or Islamophobia. The inevitable laxity resulting from this leads surreptitiously, but inexorably, to control of the prison by the gangs. One entire wing is today considered unsafe, and the guards go there reluctantly.

The government considers that the guards at Whitemoor should receive specific training on Islamic culture, to better understand the prisoners and have joint meetings for discussion on prison life and other more general topics. In another prison, guards were forbidden to wear the cross of St. George on their uniform ties, to avoid offending the sensibilities of Muslim detainees.

Most Muslims are detained for reasons unrelated to terrorism, but they spend their time alongside other prisoners with links to Al-Qaeda—and thus the prison system has become a recruiting ground for Islamic fundamentalists. This threat of radicalization is not only affecting British prisons, but other European countries, the USA, and Australia besides.[109]

3 - Czech Republic

"The prison problem is, in my opinion, a time bomb; Czech prisons are controlled by the Russian Mafia and the occurrence of a serious incident is only a matter of time." These are the words of Marie Benesova, former State Prosecutor General.[110] She added that during her time as a lawyer, a client had told her that in the prison at Bory, Plzen, inmates were able to obtain "everything they wanted"—telephones, drugs, sex and alcohol. In exchange for money, of course.

The threat is taken very seriously in the Czech Republic under the authority of a ministerial Interior Justice committee. The fight against prison gangs is jointly entrusted to the "Security Intelligence Service" (BIS) and the "Organized Crime Investigation Unit" (UOOZ) in close cooperation with the prison administration. Upon taking office as Minister of Justice in July 2002, Pavel Rychetsky,[111] declared that "putting these prison gangs in their place" would be the first of his tasks.

---

[107] McNally, M. *Muslim Gangs Taking Over British Prisons*. Report, Whitemoor Prison, June 1, 2008.

[108] Black and ethnic minority.

[109] For example, Perry, M. "Australia breaks up Muslim Prison Gang." Reuters, April 23, 2007.

[110] *Mladá fronta DNES*. July 24, 2002.

[111] Current President of the Constitutional Court of the Czech Republic. Minister of Justice from 2002 to 2003.

4 - Scandinavia

The Scandinavian countries have long considered themselves the champions of a humane approach to imprisonment and the treatment of prisoners.[112] However, today we see barbed wire surrounding high security facilities, where ten years ago there were no fences at all.

For Swedish officials, this situation is a direct consequence of prison gang activity[113] including groups called the *Brödraskapet* (or the "Wolfpack Brotherhood")[114] and the Original Gangsters. They are responsible for drug trafficking and pervasive violence, among other things. The "Original Gangsters" (OG) gang was created by Denho Acar in Gothenburg in 1993. Born in 1974, he arrived in Sweden with his family in 1985. Acar was convicted of armed robbery in 1994. He took advantage of his stay in prison to recruit new members and forge ties with the Brödraskapet. The OG has some one hundred members, mostly in the Gothenburg area, involved in affairs of extortion, robbery, drugs and murder. The gang was in conflict with the Bandidos MC and the Naserligan gang.[115] In 2006, Acar fled Sweden to avoid prosecution for arson. He carried out his military service in Turkey[116] while continuing to lead his gang via contacts with men he trusted.

In Sweden, there had never been a murder in prison until 1993, when a prisoner was stabbed in a maximum security area. Between 1993 and 2003, five other murders were committed[117] and today violence is endemic in prisons; this explains the increasingly harsh measures that the authorities have taken, albeit reluctantly. In August 2008, the Swedish magazine Expressen[118] published a list of thirteen criminals thought to be the main organized crime bosses in Sweden. Among them were four prison gang members: Geofrey Kitutu, 34, leader of the Original Gangsters, already convicted of drug and weapons offenses; Jeremy Kazcynski, 25, leader of the "15–7" gang,[119] linked to the Original Gangsters, who was arrested in July 2009 for drug trafficking, but already known to the authorities for assault and robbery; Pasi Kopra, 35, Chairman of the Wolfpack Brotherhood, sentenced to life imprisonment for an attack on a Public Prosecutor, and Denho Dano Acar. The latter recently had his residence permit revoked by the Swedish immigration authorities and his new situation may change the direction of the Original Gangsters.[120]

---

[112] Fouche, Gwladys. "Where convicts lead the good life." *Global Post*, October 19, 2009.

[113] First, the extension of outside groups, such as outlawed motorcycle gangs, mainly the Hells Angels and the Bandidos, now supplanted by bands of immigrants from the suburbs of major cities, according to a Prison Service and Parole Board report from 2001.

[114] The largest prison gang in Sweden.

[115] Composed of Macedonians and Albanians.

[116] He kept his original nationality.

[117] Karl Ritter. AP, June 8, 2003.

[118] *Expressen*, August 29, 2008

[119] 15th and 7th letters of the alphabet, O.G.

[120] *Expressen*, October 17, 2009.

In Finland, the authorities have identified seven local criminal organizations posing serious security problems. Among them is one prison gang called MORE.[121]

F - Turkey

The "high security" prison at Kartal, Istanbul, serves as headquarters for various criminal groups, as has been revealed by two letters written by mafia boss Alaattin Cakici, a former member of the Grey Wolves,[122] to two leaders of the *Karagümrük Gang*[123] Nuri and Vedat Ergin[124].The Ergin brothers had "sent" a mobile phone to Alaattin Cakici, as a gift. In his letter of thanks, Cakici proposed to share the same cell with the Ergin brothers, "to organize our affairs more effectively." Cakici also complained that the isolation he had experienced during his incarceration in France[125] had made it "impossible to take care of his criminal enterprise in Turkey." He therefore proposed an alliance with leaders of the Karagümrük gang.

These letters were later published by lawyers for the Ergin brothers, angered by rumors of conflict between the two mafia clans. The authorities found the mobile phone in Çakici's cell and confiscated it. Two weeks later, the guards found yet another. To avoid an escalation of the conflict, the prison administration then transferred Çakici to Kandira Prison in Kocaeli.[126]

G - New Zealand

In 2001 Dean Waka Nathan, 42, member of the motorcycle gang Highway 61, was jailed for life in Christchurch prison for the murder of a member of the Black Power gang. He was charged with drug trafficking from his cell and pleaded guilty. His business involved methamphetamine and cannabis movements between Auckland and Christchurch. Eight other people were arrested in this affair, dubbed Operation Fudge.[127]

The criminologist needs, therefore, to analyze this very specific threat, of which we have laid out the symptoms, in order to alert the parties involved, and explain to them the genuine risk of destabilization that these prison gangs pose today in the already fragile prison world. Serious reflection on our penal philosophy is clearly required.

---

[121] *Me Olemme Rikollisten Eliittiä* (We are the criminal elite), *Helsinki Times*, November 12, 2009.

[122] One of the most important criminal groups in Istanbul. See Raufer, X. *Le grand réveil des mafias*. Paris: JC Lattès, 2003, 279.

[123] Raufer. *Le grand réveil des mafias*, 280.

[124] Tuncay Ozkan, *Radikal*, March 2000.

[125] From August 1998 to December 1999. His arrest revealed links with the Turkish intelligence service and with politicians, bringing scandal down on the government and the the resignation of many ministers.

[126] Around 80 miles east of Istanbul.

[127] *New Zealand Herald*, September 25, 2009.

II - PRISON GANGS: ANATOMY OF THE THREAT

Although different from one prison system to another, prison gangs have, by necessity, a shared anatomy and a number of characteristics in common. Although we could, in a typological manner, distinguish between those that are created in prison on criminal foundations, those re-created in prison based on external structures, and those whose purpose is activist proselytism, we shall not take this approach here.

It is generally considered that prison gangs are highly selective, and demand absolute loyalty; they operate under codes, and adopt a hierarchical structure, dividing tasks and applying a military-style discipline. They employ violence and corruption systematically.

A - Selective Membership

Accession to a gang rests on selection made by the hierarchy of the organization. While specific criminal skills are generally required, ethnic criteria are often decisive.

This is the case in the US where the principal prison gangs were first created along ethnic lines: Latin Americans created the Mexican Mafia, African Americans created the Black Guerrilla Family,[128] whites, the Aryan Brotherhood,[129] and Puerto Ricans,[130] La Neta, each of which had its turn enjoying a near monopoly over its ethnic group.

Competition and pre-incarceration gang membership significantly increased the numbers of prison gangs. Under the pretext of escaping the domination of the Mexican Mafia, but also to compete with them, other Hispanics, for example, founded *Nuestra Familia*, reserved for Hispanics from Northern California.

To break free from the philosophical-political constraints of the Black Guerrilla Family, other African-American gangs emerged in prisons, their organizations based on pre-incarceration membership of Street gangs with the generic denominations Bloods and Crips.[131] These prison gangs call themselves the Consolidated Crip Organization

---

[128] Founded in 1966 in the California State Prison, San Quentin by a former member of the "Black Panthers", George L. Jackson. First known as the "Black Family" and the "Black Vanguard," it mutated into the BGF in 1971, when Jackson was killed, with two other detainees as they attempted to escape on August 21 of that year. His successor, James "Doc" Holiday (sic), formerly one of the leaders of the "Symbionese Liberation Army," gave the gang its final name.

[129] Appeared in San Quentin in the early 1960s. See below, "Codes of Conduct."

[130] Formed in 1970 in Puerto Rico, the gang first tried to stop the violence between inmates in Rio Pedras prison. It rapidly adopted a "cultural" and above all political image. The Neta's members in general belong to the revolutionary group "Los Macheteros" which campaigns for the independence of Puerto Rico and against the "colonialism" of the United States. They are principally found in prisons in the eastern United States.

[131] Bloods and Crips, originally from Los Angeles, are now spread across the United States. Within these "criminal faiths," gangs are not only autonomous but often rivals outside the prison. "Today... Crips are the number-one killer of Crips." Shakur. *Monster*. This is not the case within the prison system.

and the Blue Note Crip Organization (founded by Stanley Tookie Williams[132] and J. Pup King), as well as United Blood Nation and Bloodline. After several unsuccessful attempts to unite prisoners from the Crips or Bloods,[133] these are the most successful. These groups readily turn to Africanisms, using, for example, Swahili[134] words in their rules of conduct. They take the Mau Mau[135] as their reference and sometimes even the Mungiki.[136]

Others gather under an Islamic entity, for example *Ansar al-Muhammad* (AEM).[137] This group was founded by a certain Elmore Willie Brown, and became known to the public and the police force in 1993, when some of its members were arrested for rape, armed robbery and homicide.

Brown died in 2000, and the gang's hierarchy has since been collegial. The development of AEM in prisons was very fast. Considering themselves as "warriors," AEM members usually have a strict dress code, shaved heads and rigorous behavior.

Previous membership of political or terrorist groups may also promote amalgamation, consolidation and joint action in prison, under a kind of "prisoners of war" mentality. Such was the origin of the *Neta* in Puerto Rico.

Born on the streets, gangs are reconstituted within prisons as fast as their members are jailed. This has particularly been the case for Street Gangs from Chicago, the Latin Kings and the Gangster Disciples.[138] For these two gangs, both of whom employ strong symbolism[139] and maintain a very hierarchical organization,[140] the fact that many of their leaders are doomed to end their days inside won't get in the way of their continuing criminal activity.

---

[132] Founder of the Crips in 1970 with Raymond Lee Washington (shot in 1979). Tookie aroused wide controversy until his execution in December 2005. He campaigned in prison against gang crime, wrote books on the subject and made a very public series of acts of atonement—he was even proposed for the Nobel Prize... It was only later learned that he was a founder and one of the leaders of the Blue Note Crip Organization.

[133] For example, after an investigation involving several services, twenty three men and five women, members of the Bloods gang Tree Top Piru (TTP Bloods or Tree Top Pirettes for women) were indicted on February 25, 2008 in Baltimore. This gang, created in 1999 in a detention center in order to organize mutual protection against other inmates, is directly related to the Piru Bloods of Compton, California. The defendants are accused of five murders, armed robbery, drug trafficking, weapons possession and witness intimidation. Initiation rites included committing a violent crime (assault, robbery or carjacking) and submitting to a beating by other members. Members are primarily recruited in the prisons of Maryland. Steve Willock, leader of the gang, took office from his prison cell between 2000 and 2003.

[134] One of the major languages of Africa spoken from the East coast (Kenya, Tanzania) to the Great Lakes region and the eastern Democratic Republic of Congo.

[135] An anti-British rebellion movement in Kenya, active between 1952 and 1960.

[136] A politico-religious-criminal group in Kenya, banned by the government, which considers itself the heir to the Mau Mau.

[137] The Servants of Muhammad.

[138] Also known as the Black Gangster Disciples, Black Gangster Disciple Nation, and the Brothers of Struggle.

[139] Essentially a crown with five points for the Latin Kings and a three-pronged fork for the Gangster Disciples.

[140] The leaders are "Kings," "Dukes," "Counts" etc.

The criteria for recruitment have also evolved according to the intensity with which groups have been repressed. Nuestra Familia, which originally recruited its members openly and carried out its activity in prisons conspicuously, has been confronted with active federal prosecutions, threatening its survival.

Membership may also be based on a community of skills or focus of interest. The Number gangs in South Africa are not based on ethnic criteria, but are distinguished by their purpose, which others must respect. The 28s, for example, protect and organize the "camp" and manage the *wyfies* who must perform the "housework"; its combat units "use blood and poison" The 26s "find money, and steal money with patience and cunning." The 27s "enforce the codes."

The Big 5 "cooperates with the authorities to try to obtain maximum benefits" while the prime purpose of the Airforce is to organize collective escapes. Two prison gangs stand out for their "hours of business," based on tradition: The 28s, the "men of the night" are symbolized by a setting sun, while the 26s operate by day and "shall never draw blood after nightfall" except in self-defense. Their symbol is a rising sun.

Despite these differences, the Number cooperate in certain tasks. Among the most important are:

Education, for members to acquire the knowledge, experience and equipment required to adapt to their prescribed roles, and to progress in the hierarchy of their gang;

Security: by which gangs mean the protection of their members against outside danger. Members are prepared to defend the territory of their gang with their lives if necessary. Many inmates join the first gang that promises them security;

The satisfaction of physical, psychological and social needs: the Number work to obtain favorable positions within the prison in order to acquire and store desired products such as food, tobacco, drugs, and alcohol. Gangs also provide their members with camaraderie, status, protection and, in the case of the 28s, homosexual relations.

These prison gangs recruit from newcomers by entrapment or other forms of coercion, with an eye on inmates with desired qualities or skills.[141] Not belonging to a gang exposes a prisoner to beatings, rape or stabbing.

B - Loyalty

Loyalty to the group is expressed almost everywhere by the formula "Blood in, Blood out." The conditions for entry are bloodshed or killing. Membership is for life.[142] Any betrayal, or any attempt to quit the gang, lead to the only penalty in force in most criminal organizations, which is death.[143]

---

[141] Haysom, *Towards an Understanding of Prison Gangs*, 30. He states that while membership is "voluntary," some join the gang because they have been raped and prostituted, or expressly to escape this fate...

[142] Venter, Z. Just get it over with and give me my life, November, http://www.iol.co.za/news/south-africa/just-get-it-over-with-and-give-me-life-1.31222.

[143] The "Constitution" of Nuestra Familia, Article 2, paragraph 5, states that "... the death penalty will be automatic for any *familiano* who betrays, shows cowardice or deserts." Cited in the indictment of Nuestra Familia members, April 13, 2001.

"From today, you are no longer a *frans*. You're a 28. You do not insult your brothers. You do not wrong them. You never do anything that might harm your camp [gang]. And if you desert, you will do so at the price of your own blood."[144] This was corroborated by a "general" of the Airforce Gang of South Africa, before the High Court of Pretoria. Francois Van Staden,[145] 39 at the time, had been incarcerated for the first time at fourteen years of age and had spent most of his life in prison. He admitted having "executed" one of his "soldiers" who had behaved as a "rat" He revealed to the authorities that his "superior" had a pass, which opened all the doors of the facility. "We charged him with treason. There is only one sentence and that is death—he poisoned our organization. That was my role" said Francois Van Staden. He had to wait three years before the "execution" could be carried out as the victim, who felt threatened, had been transferred to another facility.

Note that although he considered himself leader of the gang in his prison, he recognizes that he would have been killed himself if he had not carried out the sentence, and that he even regarded the victim as a close "friend." He added, showing the Court the "flag" tattoo of the gang on his ankle: "The only way out of the gang is in a coffin."[146] As an illustration, a cleaner at the juvenile detention center in Pollsmoor prison, formerly a leader of the 28s, subsequently worked with the center's administration to report potentially dangerous situations. He was stabbed by inmates who saw him as a "sell-out, to be eliminated."[147]

The expression of loyalty and fidelity required of members is also a form of protection of the organization against attempts at infiltration by undercover agents or informants. The blood criterion for membership removes any doubt about the applicant, and confirms his credibility in the eyes of the leaders: "...when a member has killed, he will not reveal to the authorities acts of violence he has seen."[148]

Initiation rites always involve violence. One inmate describes his recruitment to the 28s thus: "I answered the question correctly then they told me that to join the gang I had to stab a white guard. They told me when the knife would come, how I should go about it and what I should do next."[149] Under these conditions, as long as the perpetrator is neither arrested nor recognized, this act definitively binds him to the organization for which he did the deed.[150]

---

[144] Steinberg. *Nongoloza's Children*, 22.

[145] iafrica.com, November 19, 2002.

[146] South African Press Association (SAPA), November 19, 2002.

[147] Correctional Services Portfolio Committee, Department of Regional Commissioners, Briefings August 27, 2004 (http://www.png.org.za/docs/2004/viewminute.php?id=4372).

[148] Walker, Robert. *Gangs Or Us*. 2003. www.gangsorus.com

[149] Steinberg. *Nongoloza's Children*. 28.

[150] Maughan, Karyn. "Gang Initiation Drove Man to Edge of Reason." *Cape Argus*, March 26, 2004.

C - Hierarchical Structure

For reasons of cohesion, discipline and secrecy (sometimes with the opposite effect), prison gangs operate according to hierarchies and chains of command in the military mold. Some even have ranks and are divided into units. Right from the outset, Nuestra Familia adopted a military structure with a system of ranks—generals, captains, sergeants and soldiers. However, this structure, meant to ensure efficiency and discipline, proved to be a weakness for the organization by revealing its organized nature and showing the scope of its ramifications beyond the territory of a single State. NF thus fell within the scope of the RICO law,[151] and has been subject to federal prosecution. Following this, NF was obliged to change, dividing into an "official" structure called *Nuestra Raza*,[152] operating both inside and outside the prisons. The surviving core of leaders sank into a strictly prison-based twilight, while maintaining overall control. The recruitment criteria were then changed. The "classic" prisoner in search of protection is led toward Nuestra Raza, while only the "professionals," hardened prisoners trained in discretion, almost always based on blackmail,[153] can join Nuestra Familia.

The militarized model has thus shown its limits and internal contradictions with the requirement of secrecy: Nuestra Familia was severely affected, almost destroyed, because each level knew the names of its superiors and subordinates along with the overall objectives of the organization. When it was rebuilt, it adopted a partitioned structure, better able to guarantee its security. It has an "intelligence service", the Regimental Security Department.... it appears that military references are difficult to shake off.

This pyramidal structure is also found elsewhere, for example in one of the major Taiwanese triads,[154] the *Tien Dao Man*,[155] which originated in a prison intended for the rehabilitation of prisoners through "military training."[156] From there, this prison gang developed its criminal activity throughout the island's prison world and well beyond its walls. Strongly hierarchical, in the image of the Chinese triads, but perhaps also because of its origins, Tien Dao Man[157] was formed of six "territorial"

---

[151] Racketeer Influenced and Corrupt Organizations Act (RICO): An important legal instrument in the fight against organized crime in the United States. This law allows a criminal group to be prosecuted as such for committing crimes but also for its purpose—organized crime—alone. The notion of "racket" (necessary for the implementation of this Act) includes the following offenses: death threats, kidnapping, clandestine gambling, arson, theft, robbery, extortion, corruption, forgery, bribery, obstruction of justice, racketeering (in the strict sense), prostitution, drug production and dealing.

[152] "Our race," to signal its Chicano origins. Its "official" name is the *Carnales Estructura Norteña* (Brothers of the Northern Structure), commonly known as the Northern Structure.

[153] To join, the candidate must commit a murder under orders. The sponsor knows the culprit, and through intimidation, ensures his loyalty.

[154] Along with the Bamboo Union, the Four Seas and the Pine Union.

[155] Also the "Tiendaomeng."

[156] October 1986, at the Green Island Penitentiary.

[157] Officially disbanded in 1999 "at the request" of the Taiwanese Minister of Justice. *Taipei Times*, November 11, 2001.

divisions and a general staff, presided over by the presumed boss of the organization.[158] Each subdivision had a boss, a deputy, captains and assistant captains. The number of "soldiers" in each of the subdivisions was unlimited.

Also quasi-military in their hierarchical organization are the Prison Gangs of South Africa, whose members wear imaginary colored "uniforms," hoist flags and respectfully salute each other. The fictive uniform is given to the new member at his induction ceremony: "I give you your uniform. You have a pair of white sandals. Your socks are also white, with the emblem of 28 embroidered inside and out. You wear a white shirt and a white belt with a silver buckle. You have a white tunic with two buttons, with the emblem of 28 embroidered on the inside and out. Your tie is green. Your jacket is white, also with two buttons, the first open, because you belong to the gang day and night, the second closed as a sign of discipline. You have a white beret with a silver badge engraved with a hammer and a handkerchief."[159]

The hierarchy of the 28s is rather complex: officers are called "No. 1," "judges" have eight stars, "generals" six, "colonels" four, transmission specialists, also called "number-one captains" three, "doctors" have six bars—three gold and three silver, etc. When an "officer" is transferred to another prison, he identifies himself by revealing his "uniform"—by describing in detail what he is supposed to be wearing. Each grade has a specific mission, technically defined.

Conversely, the "hard core" of the Mexican Mafia in California has no known formal hierarchy,[160] reproducing rather the "galactic" structural model of the Hispanic Gangs of East Los Angeles. Its leaders base their power on brutality, fear and the "respect" they inspire in the *carnales*, and the charismatic hold they exert upon them.[161] Their "status" is based on the crimes they have committed and their reputation; any "progression" is dependent on the violent acts they have committed. In most prisons one, sometimes two of the leaders of the Eme, are recognized as such and revered by all inmates.[162]

---

[158] Presumed to be Lo Fo-Chu, a former independent elected legislator, imprisoned in Green Island when the group was created. The Tien Dao Man claims him as one of theirs, and his name is quoted extensively in connection with shady dealings by the Taiwanese press. Lo Fu-chu was arrested in February 2002 after being added to the most-wanted list the previous January. He was sentenced on September 26, 2003 to four years in prison for corruption, fraud, breach of trust, usury, misappropriation of funds, forgery and the use of forgeries. *Taipei Times*, September 26, 2003.

[159] Steinberg. *Nongoloza's Children*, 22

[160] In some states, notably in the Texas branch of the organization, it seems that "ranks" have existed for some time. "Jury convicts Texas Mexican Mafia Sergeant in Racketeering Case." U.S. Department of Justice, U.S. Attorney's Office, Southern District of Texas. Press Release, May 23, 2003.

[161] In July 2009 the author of this article met "Boxer" Rene Enriquez, a "repentant" member of the *Eme*, formerly a high-ranking official within the organization, and author of The Black Hand (Harper Collins, September 2008). Besides an obvious charisma, he showed evidence of education, well-constructed verbal discourse and a clear vision of the activity of the Eme, which revealed a sophisticated and effective system. It was thus possible to gain a genuine understanding of the influence of these leaders over their subordinates within the organization.

[162] This falls into an "elitist" logic, reminiscent of the Russian *vory v zakones*. See An Exception, Prison Culture in Russia.

D - Code of Conduct

All prison gangs operate under a more or less formal code of conduct with rules given the status of "philosophical" principles. Adherence to this code is always manifested by a solemn oath of loyalty.

In the US, not all prison gangs have adopted the same model. The Marxist-Leninist Black Guerrilla Family is probably the most politicized US prison gang. The objectives of the BGF are "to eradicate racism, fight to maintain dignity in prison and overthrow the government." The BGF demands an oath of loyalty inspired by both Mao Zedong and the Bible, glorifying brotherhood and giving special status to group cohesion.[163]

---

[163] If I should ever break my stride, and falter at my comrades' side, This oath will kill me. If ever my world should prove untrue, should I betray this chosen few, This oath will kill me. Should I be slow to take a stand, should I show fear to any man, This oath will kill me. Should I grow lax in discipline, or in time of strife, refuse my hand, This oath will kill me. Long live comrade George Jackson! Long live the Black Guerrilla Family

[164] With reference to the letter "N,"14th letter of the alphabet, for North.

1. All Nortenos will strive for a better education, respect and social status of equality. This includes and goes beyond acquiring any incentives and privileges to which an inmate is entitled.
2. All Nortenos will take a strong positive attitude toward aiding and assisting all those of Latindescent, as well as any other minority group worthy of our cause. It is our duty to work together in harmony and unite those forces in alliance with us to reach our set goals.
3. All Nortenos will do everything within their reach and capability to acquire mainline status, for these are the grounds we must secure for our fellow Nortenos and all those who live for the cause to have a strong establishment pinta to go to, without the threat or interference of the opposition.
4. In order to continue our struggle with far less difficulties, there shall be no tolerance created by internal confrontation, individualism or homeboy favouritism. No Norteno will spread false rumors or negative gossip about a fellow Norteno, and at no time will a Norteno attempt to take advantage of, or disrespect, a fellow Norteno's ruca or familia. To do so will result in serious repercussions.
5. All Nortenos will acknowledge and respect the authority in charge at all times. No Norteno will feel inferior to one who holds rank or position. Nor will a Norteno holding rank or a position of some type feel superior to his fellow Nortenos because of his status.
6. And all data pertaining to a new arrival shall be reported through its proper channels immediately. See Household Procedures, especially that which endangers a life or is contrary to the cause.
7. At no time will a Norteno endanger the life of a fellow Norteno. There shall be no fighting amongst Nortenos, nor shall any cowardice dealing with the K-9 or enemy be tolerated. To do so will be dealt with accordingly.
8. No Norteno will lie or boast about his status. Be he rank or file, he will pay high regard to his physical and mental wellbeing and will always strive to better himself and become more aware and educated in all aspects relevant to the accomplishment of our set goals.
9. Should a Norteno be transferred from one facility to another, it is his sole duty to establish a branch in in union to procedures set henceforth and work hand-in-hand with other Nortenos at said facility and in parallel with other pintas.
10. Every chapter and stronghold of Nortenos will keep track of all enemies and enemy activities behind enemy lines.

Nuestra Raza, the "legal face" of Nuestra Familia, applies a fourteen-point manifesto[164] written by its highest officials, who intend to keep a very tight control over those they mastermind. The Diamond Tooth, later known as the Bluebird gang, became a fully-fledged prison gang in 1968[165] as the Aryan Brotherhood. Only one profession of faith is known of in its rituals, that which urges its members to brotherhood, pride and loyalty.[166] We also know that the AB is led by a pyramid of triumvirates at national and state level.

While the Mexican Mafia has no formal constitution, it nevertheless imposes specific rules. A document seized in 1996 during a search of cells contained a kind of "code" consisting of twenty-nine rules to be observed by the *Sureños*,[167] the prison population over which the Eme holds sway. This code is practical in nature, in contrast to other more political or philosophical codes.

Its provisions range from forbidding "brothers" to fight among themselves, the obligation to exercise at least 30 minutes every day, precautions to be taken when telephoning, the allocation of cells, and the circulation of intelligence to the terms of payment for clandestine goods. The rules are inculcated to newcomers and strictly observed; they even provide for a three strikes[168] penal system copied from precisely the principle that led so many members of the Eme to end up in jail, with one small difference—a third offense is, as always in this world, punishable by death.

The Gangster Disciples have a centralized and hierarchical structure, not only having a long written constitution, but also codes and rules for membership and behavior; they regularly circulate "memos" in the prisons they dominate, often "reminders of the rules." They also use "application forms" which applicants must fill out in great detail in order to have their background checked out.

---

11. It is each Norteno's responsibility that is aware of our struggle to teach and school all those destined for the pinta. No Norteno should enter the pinta blind or without knowledge of our struggle behind the walls.
12. A Norteno will protect and defend his household to the fullest, no matter the circumstances or consequences. This means closing ranks with fellow Nortenos during battle. To abandon such responsibilities will be considered as an act of treason.
13. A Norteno leaving for the streets is encouraged to assist his fellow Nortenos behind the walls in whatever form or fashion he may choose. This is not mandatory but is a step towards the elite circle of dedicated Norteno Soldados.
14. A Norteno shall stay abreast of all new laws, policies and procedures. No portion of this format is to be misinterpreted or abused for personal gain. To do so will be considered as an act of treason.

[165] That is to say when, in the eyes of the prison authorities, it has attained a "sufficient" level of organization and capacity for harm, which goes beyond the simple level of "disturbance."

[166] "An Aryan brother is without a care/He walks where the weak and heartless won't dare/And if by chance he should stumble, and lose control/His brothers will be there, to help reach is goal/For a worthy brother, no need is too great/He need not but ask, fulfillment's his fate/For an Aryan brother, death holds no fear/Vengeance will be his, through his brothers still here."

[167] Hispanics from Southern California originally, and by extension all those in the rest of the United States, identify with the Eme.

[168] Three Strikes and you're out, US laws removing from society third offenders, those considered as "professional criminals," with the imposition of a very long sentence.

While the rules are usually in written form in US Prison Gangs, they are transmitted by oral tradition in South Africa. Despite the antiquity of these organizations, their original values seem to have remained intact. Each one has its disciplinary code, provisions for various punishments, symbols, hierarchical organization and specific modes of promotion.[169] Finally, the historical interface between the various gangs also seems to have persisted. Among these rules, there is one that demands use of the Number's prison language, called *Sabela*. The "Mambozas"[170] decide when to teach Sabela to a new prospect, and "it is a long and painful process."[171] "Your 'blackboard' [teacher] will speak Sabela day and night. During your first two months in the gang, you will receive no visits, neither read nor write letters nor read books. You must focus on the gang, and if you are too slow to learn, you are punished severely. If you cannot seem to remember something that you were taught, you are stripped and placed under cold water in the shower until your memory comes back."[172]

The PCC in Brazil has a code.[173] It was discovered when copies were found on two members arrested during the events of 2006. It consists of seventeen sections specifying the organization of the group and its activities. It reveals the relationship between the gang and the *Commando Vermelho* in Rio. The code, which calls for a "war without truce and without borders until final victory," provides for the "death penalty" for any breach of the rules as laid down; it ends with a political affirmation, "Freedom, Justice and Peace."

E - Violence and Intimidation

"These gangs extort, steal, use and sell drugs. There are always ten of them to attack one inmate. They use terror to persuade others to give them their property, their money, everything they own; they set fire to the cells of those who resist them and barricade their own to protect their "goods." They make weapons and beat other inmates. Every week, three in five detainees request protection—at least as many again are soundly beaten or stabbed. The guards are afraid to pass through the corridors housing these violent prisoners. Do not let those you speak to underestimate the phenomenon of prison gangs and their criminal activities."[174] A prisoner's letter to the Secretary of Prisons in New Mexico provides an example of the influence prison gangs have on prison life.

This same violence is corroborated by a member of the Texas Mexican Mafia,[175] sentenced to sixty years at the age of 17: "When the Gang recruited me in 1990, the

169 Haysom, *Towards an Understanding of Prison Gangs*.
170 The "forties," a sort of council of elders, not criminally active in prisons.
171 Steinberg, *Nongoloza's Children*, 24.
172 Steinberg, *Nongoloza's Children*, 24.
173 *Estatudo do PCC* (in Portuguese): http://www1.folha.uol.com.br/folha/cotidiano/ult95u22521.shtml
174 News & Opinion. "Making Prisons Safe." *Albuquerque Weekly Alibi*, June 14, 1999.
175 Also known as the *Mexikanemi*, meaning "long live the people of Mexico." The Texas branch of the Eme, enjoying a certain autonomy and a separate organization, in particular awards ranks.

Texas Mafia became my God. It had started this violent and murderous war with the Aryan Brotherhood. My penchant for violence and brutality quickly gave me a place in the gang and I got a reputation throughout the prison system in Texas pretty quick. By 18, I'd been promoted to lieutenant, after being in on one serious punishment of another prisoner who had talked about the Texas Mafia to outsiders... At 20, I had reached the rank of captain in one of the deadliest prison gangs. I was totally contaminated by their way of thinking... I was sent to the McConnell Unit in Beeville, Texas, later known as the "hate factory." In that corrupted world gangs ruled. Violence, rape, murder, homosexuality and extortion were a way of life. It was paradise for me. At McConnell, I began to build my own system of perverse and violent power. At my discretion, men were bought, sold, prostituted or beaten. This power blinded me so much I really started to believe I could take on the system and win."[176]

In a closed universe, violence and intimidation are the weapons of choice for prison gangs. They compromise the safety of other inmates and that of the prison staff. The whole institution and its surroundings are concerned.

We have seen how extreme violence led the Nuova Camorra Organizzata to ruin. Yet this is the usual way of gaining power, both individually and collectively, within the prison world. It is also the normal mode of conflict resolution, even in its most perverse forms such as the slow puncture method mentioned above.

In December 1972, the murder of Rudy Cheyenne Cadena,[177] charismatic leader of the Mexican Mafia in Chino prison[178] resulted in thirty murders in the prison world in the following weeks.[179] This "vendetta" is still ongoing and, according to experts, has caused more than a thousand deaths over the years within the prison system and in the streets.

Violence between members and non-members is common in South Africa, while violence within a gang is exceptional and only occurs in specific circumstances, where a member has breached the code. For example, although the 28s and 26s frequently oppose each other, a certain respect remains. None, for example, would authorize an inmate who committed an offense against a member of another gang to join their own gang before the wrong had been righted.

In this context, the ability to fight and the nature of the crime committed confer a status within the prison with a threefold objective:[180] it demonstrates the passage from boyhood to manhood; it is used to mark the boundary between the space of the gang and that of the guards; finally, it divides inmates into men and *wyfies*.

---

[176] Smedley, Henry. *My Life in Prison Gangs*. Denver, CO: Bible Advocate Press, 2000.

[177] The character of "Cheyenne" inspired the 1992 Edward James Olmos movie "American Me." Shot in the district of Ramona Gardens, East LA, the movie cost the lives of several people who agreed to advise its producers, including a social worker, Ana Lizarraga (killed June 14, 1993), because certain scenes offended the Mexican Mafia. Olmos himself was the victim of threats and blackmail.

[178] Seventy miles east of Los Angeles.

[179] *Gang Beat* 12, 4, Summer 2001.

[180] Steinberg. *Nongoloza's Children*.

Violence may be controlled or spontaneous. For example, on January 4, 2015, while he was assaulting a guard as part of his initiation rite in the South African prison at Blandvlei,[181] northeast of Cape Town, a detainee was killed by other guards.[182] In retaliation, it seems, nine guards were then attacked and injured with knives by inmates at Darkenstein prison,[183] twenty-five miles to the west. The attackers were all members of Number gangs, the 26s, 27s and 28s.

Violent acts occasionally serve other objectives. Prisoners have been known to attack guards just to stay in prison. These rare incidents are not related to the activities of prison gangs or any initiation rite, but are rather the result of the extreme poverty in which detainees would find themselves if they left prison. For them, despite the deprivation of liberty, the living conditions and the abuses they face, prison is the lesser evil.[184]

Violence also serves to punish. Besides the slow puncture, mentioned above, which is a recent introduction, the Number chastise their own members in less serious cases with a punishment previously used by prison staff, called the "carry-on." Whoever is at fault is made to stand, shirtless, arms raised. The punishment squad forms a circle around him, and when one of them calls "Up" the others beat his chest with socks containing blunt objects.

Due to its slow recovery from the operations carried out in 2006, the PCC seems to have returned to its preferred methods, threatening or killing prison guards to intimidate the authorities in order to gain concessions.[185] Such has been shown by arrests made in 2007, like others before them. Three people were arrested on February 7 of that year in possession of the names and private addresses of twenty prison officers, of whom ten worked in Presidente Bernardes prison, where Marcola, supreme leader of the PCC is held. The suspects were members of the PCC, with a mission to assassinate these guards in reprisal for the recent transfer of PCC leaders from a less secure prison to the Bernardes Penitentiary Rehabilitation Center. The murders were not carried out, those who were to commit them were arrested—no doubt the authorities were warned by wire taps—but everything indicates that the violence persists. If the plan had succeeded, no one, neither authorities nor the PCC itself, can imagine what the consequences might have been.

III - PRISON GANGS: PATHOGENESIS

The pathogenesis of prison gangs has three aspects.

First, they hold the power of life and death over individuals within the closed prison world, according to their own criteria and rules that differ depending on the institution, the security measures in place and the country.

---

[181] At Worcester, Cape Province.

[182] IOL News, January 23, 2015.

[183] At Southern Paarl, Cape Province.

[184] Joseph, Norman. "Inmates Attack Warders to Stay in Prison." *Cape Argus*, May 14, 2004, 8.

[185] Steinberg. *Nongoloza's Children*, 15.

Secondly, these groups organize and manage the traffic upon which life inside the prison is based. Everything has a price inside—both people and things. Almost everything is in short supply, and every possession becomes an instrument of power. The control of drugs, cigarettes, alcohol and sex by prison gangs confers far higher authority than any legitimate governance.

Finally, communication with the outside world, largely facilitated by modern technology,[186] but still working through intimidation and corruption, allows the leaders of these gangs to manage their criminal "businesses" from the inside.

Tightly protected, these individuals have the best means of persuasion possible, the choice between money and death, *plata o plomo*, according to the Colombian saying from Escobar's time. It has led inexorably to the influence of prison life extending ever farther beyond the prison walls into society at large.

A - Inside

Born in the prison world and enjoying a guarantee of sustainability, prison gangs will prevail even in establishments where, in theory, security—control and isolation—is strongest.

1 - Control of Prison Life

In all prisons in the world, any newcomer is immediately challenged and judged. His behavior from the first moment will determine his entire sentence. He can face up to it and fight, pay for protection, or become a slave. He may also be required to provide "proof" of his previous criminal activities, which will be carefully checked. Unless he has proven support or his own means, the prisoner cannot hope to avoid the dead weight of prison logic: he must either belong to an organization or be exploited by it.

The prisoner with no gang membership or who cannot pay the price of his protection becomes a slave. The only rule is that of the strongest. The need to seek a place in the group and to submit to its "laws" is therefore an imperative; failure to respect these carries only one penalty and that is death.

An anecdote may show the control that prison gangs are able to exercise and the competition they engage in, one against the other. Ian Huntley, the killer of two ten year old girls in Soham, near Cambridge, England, was sentenced and imprisoned in December 2003. In May 2004 a rumor was heard that he had become the subject of a competition between two prison gangs. The winner was to be the gang who executed him after disfiguring him by scalding, as an expression of contempt. Bets were widely placed at Wakefield Prison, passions raged about which of the two gangs would win. According to a prisoner interviewed by a newspaper (one wonders how),

[186] See box "Mobile phones and prisons."

"it will be surprising if Huntley is still alive in a year."[187] He is still alive at the time of writing. It appears that certain informants, exchanging information for favors, warned the authorities, who were very keen to avoid a repeat of the January 2004 "suicide" of Harold Shipman, the famous "Doctor Death."[188] The affair was taken extremely seriously. Huntley's guard was doubled and placed on high alert. He was eventually transferred to another facility.

The impact of prison gangs on the inmate's life is proportional to the ambient violence of the institution, itself a function of the "security level" of the prison. Paradoxically, prison gangs are more present, more powerful and more violent where "security" is the highest, and control the strictest. Conversely, they have less influence in open prisons.

The leaders of prison gangs often enjoy various privileges, as much in terms of their comfort inside as in access to the facilities they need to pursue their criminal activities, as we saw in the case of Raffaele Cutolo, head of the Nuova Camorra Organizzata.

According to the country concerned, the era in question, and the particular circumstances, governors and prison administrators have often considered prison gangs to be stable elements with which business might be done. They have seen in them a guarantee of peace for their institution, a way to avoid the kind of violent incidents that might cast a cloud over their careers.

In Brazil, Colombia, Venezuela and Honduras, the tradition is for directors of penitentiaries to entertain relationships with prisoners' associations—at least with the most "legitimate" among them—but this has tended to disappear with the advent of the trafficking and violence associated with more recently emergent groups.

In the US, one of the leaders of the Latin Kings, Fernando Zayas, nicknamed Prince Fernie, imprisoned for a triple murder, worked as a plumber and painter in Stateville prison, a position that allowed him to move freely throughout the facility, maintaining contacts and developing his trafficking networks. Robert Big Lowe, a leader of the Gangster Disciples, would only move about in prison with his bodyguards and always carried a leather briefcase, the contents of which remained a mystery to everyone. He had his own cook and two cells, one for living, one for storage of food and goods smuggled in from outside. Why all this? Big Lowe was feared by the prison administration—he was believed to be behind a riot that had killed three guards.[189]

When the cell of Ernest "Smokey" Wilson, another leader of the Gangster Disciples, was searched, they found "a mobile phone, four batteries, thirteen bottles of luxury cologne, a mini-TV, an electric iron, two kettles and a portable washing

[187] *Daily Mirror*, May 24, 2004.

[188] BBC News online http://news.bbc.co.uk/2/hi/uk/3391897.stm BBC News online http://news.bbc.co.uk/2/hi/uk/3391897.stm

[189] At Pontiac, in 1978, according to M. Heltsley, former member of the prison administration, quoted in the ERRI Special Report, 1997. Lowe shares this reputation with Larry "King" Hoover, cited below. See Knox, George W. *The Gangster Disciples: a gang profile*. Peotone, IL: National Gang Crime Research Center, (Published on the Internet), 2000.

machine"[190] and "no-one" could understand how they might have gotten into his cell. With increasing regularity, precision electronic scales for weighing drugs are found in cells, an extremely useful device in constant use.

In institutions where prison gangs hold sway, they eventually end up governing all aspects of daily life—what prisoners eat, at what time and in what place they are to sit in the refectory, who will have the least harsh or the most tedious tasks, who will have money and luxurious clothes, who will live and who will die. All this and much more falls under the direct remit of the gangs.

For the US prison officers union, prison governors who grant privileges to the leaders of prison gangs and turn a blind eye to their activities dangerously discredit the authority structure and destabilize the entire population of the institution. This is even more the case when negotiations and long-standing agreements have resulted in "acquired rights" for prison gangs. To restore order and discipline requires a change of governance and a total restructuring of the institution.[191]

Far, then, from being stabilizing or mediating agencies, prison gangs contribute enormously to disorder and violence within prisons, through their criminal practices, the climate they create and the gross human rights violations inflicted upon the great majority of inmates. While keeping the common title of Prison Gangs, American experts now rank them in a particular category, to highlight the specific threat they represent, imposing the term "Disruptive Groups"[192] to better characterize their destabilizing nature.

Prison staff, as well as prisoners, are threatened by the activity of prison gangs. Guards may be led to participate in criminal activities, be it voluntarily or otherwise, or may themselves be victims.

For a guard, voluntary participation is to be guilty of collusion with a group—providing alibis, facilitating certain activities or certain acts of violence, being paid for silence or assistance. Involuntary participation involves a guard ignoring some wrongdoing or being willfully negligent to ensure a peaceful life for himself.

Wherever prison gangs exist, guards are potential victims. They are threatened, harassed, sometimes sexually abused and even murdered. In the US, the situation has degenerated so far that 70% of penitentiary institutions now train their staff to manage the specific hazards associated with the gangs and teach them how to behave with their members.[193]

---

[190] Emergency Response and Research Institute (ERRI), Special Report, 1997.

[191] In June 1994, for example, the prison guards union at Pontiac, Illinois, complained that the directors of the institution had signed agreements with the gangs. They demanded a "zero tolerance" policy to ensure their security in carrying out their duties.

[192] According to the Texas Commission on Law Enforcement: "Any group of prisoners which represents a threat to the physical safety of other inmates as a result of its nature and its activities." (www.tcleose.state.tx.us). The term Security Threat Groups is also used, but rather to describe groups that are not yet fully organized into Prison Gangs.

[193] Knox, George W. "A National Assessment of Gangs and Security Threat Groups (STGs) in Adult Correctional Institutions: Results of the 1999 Adult Corrections Survey." *Journal of Gang Research* 7, 3 (2000), 1–4.

In early 2003, a guard at Cameron prison, Texas, was removed from his post and charged with having brought drugs inside. In his version of events, a gang member had "threatened him with reprisals if he failed to obey orders." Also suspended was the head of security of the prison, who declared at his subordinate's trial that: "Members of the Texas Syndicate[194] threatened me with death [...] they try to manipulate everyone. If we give in on a detail they immediately go further, demanding larger and larger concessions. Then they make sure you know you're a coward for backing down, they blackmail you, threaten your job. I heard this often."[195] According to the prison hierarchy, however, most staff do not yield to threats, and affairs like that of Cameron are only "isolated cases of people looking for a quick profit."

Collusion with the prison gangs caused by greed can totally corrupt the staff of an institution. In Texas again, in 1994–95, the police dismantled a prison gang known as the Blue Bandana,[196] responsible for violence and trafficking within the prison environment. The group was composed solely of prison guards.

Control of prison life by the gangs also involves extortion and "protection." Cells are often "taxed" according to various criteria—ethnic, linguistic or corresponding to particular types of crime. Drug addicts prefer to be remote from guard posts while certain inmates want to be close to TV sets if there are any. All commodities or "comforts" have a price, fixed by the gang with jurisdiction over it.

For members of the Primero Commando da Capital in Brazil, this tax is replaced by a relatively modest monthly fee—50 Reals for those in prison and 500 for those outside.[197] Those who cannot pay are often tasked with high-risk missions such as attacks on the police to satisfy their debt. This "tax" allows the "union," which keeps a permanent treasury of at least a million dollars, to organize escapes and pay lawyers, but also to help sick inmates, and escaped or released prisoners and their families. It is a genuine cooperative organization which reflects its growing "politicization."[198]

In the United States, prisoners not belonging to a gang are often termed "neutrons." Prison gangs levy a "tax" of 10–50 dollars per month on them just to have the "right" to live in prison. Again, certain dangerous tasks are imposed upon them—smuggling drugs into the prison or hiding the gang's weapons[199] in their cells. They are

---

[194] One of the oldest Hispanic prison gangs, limited to the state of Texas and ranked second behind the Mexican Mafia by the Texas Department of Criminal Justice.

[195] *Brownsville Herald*, April 4, 2003.

[196] In the "McConnell area" of Beeville prison, Texas. "In Texas Prisons, it's Hard to Tell Who your Enemies Are." *Austin Chronicle*, April 28, 2003. Also, see the *People's Tribune* (Online Edition), 22,14, April 3, 1995. Corroborated by Smedley, *My Life in Prison Gangs*.

[197] Respectively $28 and $280 (rate on January 2010). These contributions have been halved since 2006.

[198] The PCC, from being a "Union" became the "Union of the Marginalized" in 2001.

[199] In the prison world, anything can become a weapon, and the ingenuity of prisoners is highly developed: "A 'paper pole' is a conical tube fashioned from paper, tightly rolled and sealed with tape, stuffed with toilet paper to make it hard, and fitted with a sharp point (from a ballpoint pen or a disposable razor, for example). It is delivered by hand, or launched with a piece of rubber stretched taut into a powerful slingshot. Paper poles can be fired across buildings from one block of cells to another. Inmates will fashion a makeshift knife, or shank, out of almost anything..." *Austin Chronicle*, April 28, 2003.

often prostitutes. A neutron from Menard Prison, for example, was stabbed by an enforcer[200] from the Latin Kings because he refused to conceal a weapon. Another was regularly raped for refusing to join the gang.

To better control prison life, gangs practice a division of labor according to the skills of their members and their objectives. Some act as security officers, others gather intelligence (about other gangs, the administration, and the activities of the justice department and the police). Others are in charge of physical training, while some oversee landline telephones and reserve their use for members of their organization.

How can the power that gangs hold over the prison population be explained?

The punishment they deal out—notably death—is always more severe than that legally employed by the legitimate authority of the institution. The prisoners are under no illusion that the nominal protection the prison administration is supposed to afford them has any meaning whatsoever.

The intimidation of inmates may go far beyond the prison environment. It is said, for example, that the 28 gang in South Africa "cries for eighty years." This is meant to convey that "nobody is beyond the reach of its vengeance."[201] The gang has a reputation for relentlessly hunting down traitors, which helps keep a tight rein on those who might be tempted to testify against it.[202]

Despite their proven pernicious nature, some still consider this kind of "intermediate body" to be useful or even desirable. In an article in 2014, entitled "Prison Gangs and the Community Responsibility System"[203] professors Garrett Roth[204] and David Skarbek[205] proposed to "forget the outdated image of violent and racist thugs coming together to rob the weakest..." According to them, prison gangs are "vital elements of social cohesion... allowing violence to be kept at manageable levels and creating a stable environment in which an economy based on contraband can develop."

This economic and behaviorist approach seems to forget the reality and daily life of those who, imprisoned for small crimes, see their lives ruined forever.

---

[200] A gang member charged with enforcing gang rules.

[201] On December 10, 2003, a future "soldier" of the 28s passing through the initiation phase, appeared before the High Court in Cape Town. He was accused of killing the mother of his child and his neighbor, a boy of eight, to show his determination to the gang. The mother of the girlfriend of the alleged murderer, who wished to testify, suffered intimidation for eight months by "unidentified" individuals. "No witness, no procedure," they told her. She is currently part of a witnesses protection program, and lives anonymously far from her original home. *Cape Argus*, December 10, 2003.

[202] Nonetheless, South African law requires prisoners to appear before the courts when they are summoned, refusal being punished by two additional years. The law also provides for placement in a "safe" prison. Haysom, *Towards an Understanding of Prison Gangs.*

[203] Roth, M. Garrett and David Skarbek. "Prison Gangs and the Community Responsibility System." *Review of Behavioral Economics*, 1, 3 (2014), 223–243.

[204] Oberlin College, Department of Economics.

[205] King's College London, Department of Political Economy.

2 - *Trafficking*

Alongside violence, trafficking is the other arm of the command structure in jail, as "traffic is power."[206] Inside, in an environment of deprivation, everything is trafficked, organized and controlled by criminal gangs. Certain prison gang leaders become veritable captains of industry from their prison cells. They create and maintain strong and lucrative black markets in drugs, alcohol, and tobacco. They organize gambling and prostitution—they even open restaurants in prisons. Imprisonment appears to be absolutely no obstacle to the pursuit of lucrative criminal activities.

Of these, the trade in tobacco has the longest tradition. It has often been at the origins of prison gangs themselves. The Tien Dao Man triad began its business by monopolizing the cigarette market in the prisons of Taiwan. Anyone wanting to smoke in prison had to deal with members of the triad. Cigarettes were cut in half and re-rolled to make two slimmer smokes. A pack of 24, the price of which they doubled, became a pack of 48; they thus quadrupled their income by selling them individually.[207]

In the US, recent "politically correct" bans on smoking in prisons have given cigarette trafficking a whole new lease of life. Any forbidden commodity sees its market value rise. For specialists like Cory Godwin, president of the association of Florida prison administration investigators, "banning smoking in prisons was simply crazy—who ever thought it could do anything but strengthen the gangs?"[208]

Today, the largest prison trade by far involves drugs. Beyond the huge profits made, the drug is in itself a tool of domination. The traffic causes bloody conflicts between gangs and worsens the natural instability of the prison world.

One report[209] emphasizes how widely available drugs are in Pollsmoor detention center, Cape Town. Some are brought in by staff, others by the prisoners themselves, especially when escorted by police to the court cells. In 2004, nine staff members were arrested for drug trafficking.

The prices of drugs vary at Pollsmoor, but in general, methaqualone[210] and crack cost twice as much as they do in the street. There are several reasons for this. First, smuggling drugs into prisons comes with a risk (getting caught) and is expensive (bribing the guards). Secondly, dealers can only sell inside with the permission of the gangs, who levy a large commission, shared between its members. The profit margin needs to be very high. Finally, drugs are rare in prison, and demand almost always exceeds supply.

---

[206] Cory Godwin, quoted by Tiffany Danitz, "The Gangs Behind Bars," *Insight on the News*, September 28, 1998, 1–3.

[207] *Taipei Times*, November 11, 2001.

[208] Quoted in Danitz, *The Gangs Behind Bars*.

[209] Report of the White Paper Committee on Prison Services during their visit to the juvenile detention center at Pollsmoor on October 15, 2004. (http://www.pmg.org.za/docs/2004viewminute.php).

[210] A drug that appeared in the early 1980s and became very popular in South Africa, with the common names "mandrax," "quaaludes" or "ludes." It has "relaxing, euphoric and aphrodisiac effects."

Richard Valdemar, a sergeant specializing in prison gangs at the Los Angeles Sheriff's Department, has calculated the tonnage and cash turnover associated with heroin trafficking in the prison of Los Angeles County,[211] an institution for prisoners in transit, awaiting trial or serving short sentences. Heroin is probably the least used drug in California since a number of poisoned batches were distributed around twenty years ago. Nonetheless, even given the above conditions, those who control this traffic make a substantial profit. Here are Valdemar's figures:

Average population on any given day:	18,639 prisoners
Heroin addicts (± 10% of prisoners):	1,864 prisoners
Detoxed (± 2% of addicts):	-38
Total active heroin addicts on any given day:	1,826 prisoners
Minimum daily dose of heroin:	0.01 g per user
A total each day of:	18.26 g heroin
An annual consumption of:	6664.9 g (6.7 kg)
Value of one gram:	$ 80 on the street
	$ 240 in jail
In one year, for this prison, heroin dealing *alone* yields a minimum of some:	$ 1,600,000

More than 6.5 kg of heroin is a considerable quantity. The quantities and cash traded for marijuana and cocaine are undoubtedly much higher. For example, Jimmy Delgado, a "sergeant" of the Texas Mexican Mafia, was convicted of "conspiracy, racketeering and trafficking" after dealing more than 5 kg of cocaine in the Texas prison system.[212] These are huge amounts considering the system is meant to be "closed," and proves the extraordinary resourcefulness of gangs in prison.

In 1995, 25% of inmates in US high security prisons were drug addicts. The figure is probably higher today.[213]

How do drugs make their way into prison? The complicity of corrupt guards is, of course, vital, but the wives and friends of detainees are often involved, as well as "associates" of the criminal groups—sometimes, too, women organized in gangs.[214] These women are often used as "mules," who are either voluntary, threatened or paid. They are better equipped to hide drugs about their person and are often under less suspicion than their male counterparts.

---

[211] Valdemar, R., California Prison gangs information sheet, California Gang Investigators Association, 2003.

[212] He is also accused of three murders. US Department of Justice, US Attorney's Office, Southern District of Texas, press release, May 23, 2003.

[213] Emergency Response and Research Institute. Unfortunately we were unable to find more recent figures.

[214] For example, a subgroup of the Gangster Disciples recruited young schoolgirls called the "Sisters of Struggle" or the "Intellectual Sisters." They serve as logistical support to imprisoned members of GD. The female subgroup of the Latin Kings is, of course, called the Latin Queens.

A May 2009 report[215] from the New Jersey Corrections Department revealed that insufficient checks on street gang membership when hiring prison staff had resulted in a system of corruption that allowed guards and visitors alike to bring all manner goods and objects into prison, and in very large quantities. One guard was found to have brought "incalculable" quantities of methamphetamines into the institution where she worked.

In California, "dozens of employees in recent years have been dismissed and arrested for their allegiance to gangs."[216] In 2009, for example, the prison intelligence services discovered that one prison guard was the wife of a member of the Mexican Mafia.

In Brazil carrier pigeons were trained to bring drugs to PCC members in Marilia prison, São Paulo state. An increase in drug seizures in the cells had alerted the attention of staff who were mystified as to how the traffic was getting in.

At one of his trials, it was learned that Larry King Hoover, one of the main leaders of the Gangster Disciples was managing one of the most successful cocaine distribution "companies" in the United States from prison. According to Thomas Dart, the President of the Commission in charge of prisons in the House of Representatives, Hoover was far more effective working from his cell, with its guaranteed security,[217] than he ever was after his release.

This is not surprising. According to reports from the Illinois prison administration,[218] referring to "highly placed" sources, "prison gangs have absolute control over Stateville prison, and the guards are terrorized. If they dare to stop the friends or family of gang members smuggling stuff in, the gangs produce photographs of their homes, their wives, and their children."[219]

According to these same sources, Lawrence K. appeared on a hit list drawn up by the Latin Kings[220] of thirty "bad" guards who were simply doing their job without giving in to threats or letting their integrity be compromised;[221] they were therefore impeding the gang's activities. Lawrence K., thirty years of age, was therefore murdered shortly after the appearance of a letter to staff threatening death if they refused to "facilitate" the gang's business. Among the Latin Kings, this type of execution must be ordered or

---

[215] *Gangland Behind Bars: How and Why Organized Criminal Gangs Street Thrive in New Jersey's Prisons and What Can be Done About it.* State of New Jersey Commission of Investigation, May 2009.

[216] California Department of Corrections and Rehabilitation, Special Service Unit; telephone interview, January 6, 2010. In *Gangs Infiltrating Law Enforcement and Correctional Agencies*, Intelligence Report, National Gang Intelligence Center, January 15, 2010.

[217] Hoover was once attacked by a homosexual named Nissan who wanted to humiliate him. He managed to stab him two or three times before Hoover's bodyguards intervened. Knox, *An Introduction to Gangs.*

[218] Knox, *An Introduction to Gangs.*

[219] Knox, *An Introduction to Gangs.*

[220] Their "blacklist" of people to be eliminated.

[221] "K. was the type of guard who came to work to do his job, he was young." Knox, George W. Gang profile: The Latin Kings. Peotone, IL: National Gang Crime Research Center, (Published on the Internet), 2000.

controlled by a senior leader—yet, to date, none of them has been charged. According to testimony from members of the gang who knew of the affair, Lawrence K. was probably murdered on the direct order of Lord Gino (Colon). K. and other guards reportedly found cocaine in Colon's cell. Such a brazen affront would have been unforgivable and Lawrence K.'s execution "before the day is out" would have been ordered.[222]

Another object, psychologically as important as drugs and coveted as much, is the weapon. Depending on the country and the level of sophistication of the institution involved, the nature of weapons differs. In South America guns are commonplace while knives are preferred elsewhere—but anything is possible, anywhere.[223] All prison gangs are involved in the trafficking of weapons; sometimes they form an alliance against the administration. Some prison gangs have members specialized in the supply and hiding of arms.

Besides drugs, weapons and cigarettes, any commodity may be traded in the prison world according to opportunity and resources. Each phase of the traffic is always under the control of the prison gangs, increasing their influence and power.

Prison gangs are not the only ones to take advantage of traffic inside. Guards are involved too. In Grootvlei,[224] four inmates got their hands on a mini video surveillance camera and filmed the guards[225] selling alcohol and drugs,[226] pimping out "sex slaves," and even providing a firearm (loaded) to a prisoner.[227] The most brutal scene in their movie showed a prisoner having sex with a minor who had been "delivered" to his cell by corrupt guards. The "Grootvlei Four," all condemned to heavy sentences, had taken care to film themselves negotiating drug deals with the guards. They then handed the cassettes[228] to the governor of the facility[229] who forwarded them to the Jali Commission. The case was a national scandal. The guards were suspended immediately and the governor was transferred[230] one week later. The leader of the Four, Gayton M., was released on parole two years before the end of his minimum term.[231] All four were sentenced to death by the 26 gang.[232]

---

[222] Knox. *Gang profile: The Latin Kings.*

[223] The administration of the Pontiac facility (Illinois) has never found three firearms on which it received information.

[224] At Bloemfontein, South Africa.

[225] Around twenty in number. South African Presss Association (SAPA), June 19, 2002.

[226] The specialty of one guard, who had a luxury car and a comfortable home, was the supply of brandy. He was selling ten to twenty bottles per week and earning extra income of some $1,700 per month. *Dispatch Online*, July 16, 2002.

[227] *Prison Warders Filmed Selling Drugs and Sex.* South African Press Association, June 19, 2002, citing the South African Broadcasting Corporation (SABC).

[228] Two and a half hours in total.

[229] The four inmates were placed under special protection on the same day. As soon as word got out, one of them suffered two assassination attempts.

[230] SAPA, June 26, 2002.

[231] SAPA, February 28, 2003.

[232] According to Marius Engelbrecht, a "Major" of the 26s, "They will die in prison, there is no safe place for them—not in any prison in the country." Minutes of the Jali Commission, Bloemfontein Supreme Court, June 28, 2002, 743.

3 - Corruption

Corruption often begins with relationships between prisoners and guards becoming "too close." In the UK, nearly a thousand employees are suspected of being compromised. For remuneration, they have agreed to bring mobile phones and drugs into prison, and to facilitate the transfer of detainees from one prison to another, according to a 2006 report.

Despite numerous reports indicating cases of corruption, no sanctions have ever been imposed by the administrative hierarchy. "What was presented as a handful of isolated cases of corruption is actually the emerging face of a huge iceberg of dishonest practices. In short, [the prison authorities] find themselves accused of institutional corruption at the national level."[233] The administration has been forced to recognize the existence of "a small but significant minority of unscrupulous agents"[234] but suggests that a decline in drug abuse and the number of escape attempts proves the integrity of the majority of guards. This ignores a rate of absenteeism so high among these very guards that the Prison Service is considering no longer paying sick leave.

In South Africa, in addition to the many elements that demonstrate the extent of the phenomenon, a UN team studying corruption has shown that among the different types of malpractice in which South African prison guards engage, trafficking is involved in 13% of investigations.[235]

One of the most disturbing discoveries among those made by the Jali Commission was how an official at Grootvlei prison was not only selling *dagga* and methaqualone to detainees, but even allowing them to come to his own home to buy them.

One prisoner told the Commission how he could earn around 450 Rand[236] per month selling methaqualone on behalf of his guards, and how he was enlisted because he had no relatives or visitors.

However subtle and well-organized such traffic may be, it would be virtually impossible without corruption. Those gang leaders tasked with "public relations" meet officials of the institutions discreetly and forge agreements to further their members' interests over those of other prisoners; this is even the specific function of the Big 5 Gang within the South African prison system. The arrangements do not only offer a way to live together. The huge profits made by all prison gangs make bribery of prison staff, often poorly paid, very easy.

---

[233] Mark Leech, director of *Prisons Handbook*, the annual guide for the British penal system, Belga News Agency, July 31, 2006.

[234] Phil Wheatley, Director General of the Prison Service, Belga News Agency, online since July 31, 2006.

[235] Painter-Morland, Mollie. *Final Consolidated Report - Focused Assessment of Anti-Corruption Capacity within the Department of Correctional Services.* Pretoria, Republic of South Africa: United Nations Office on Drugs and Crime, 2004.

[236] $61 in January 2010.

Without the active participation of guards[237] in the traffic, the availability of food, drugs and money within the prison would be severely restricted. One prisoner tells of an exchange between an inmate and a member of the prison staff: "If you have money you can buy anything, and if you got the guard right, you can send him out for cartons of cigarettes. If you make them happy you can even get them to bring you some Nando's[238] or whatever. To guard [young offenders], you need a lot of money, you have to sell stuff [to pay them]. There are many boys who sell drugs or dagga, all these things, and the police sell everything going."[239]

In the US, during the trial of "King" Hoover, mentioned above, a guard admitted that, like other colleagues, he earned between 500 and 1000 dollars a day bringing drugs into the prison. He added "every gang has its appointed guards—usually chosen from among those working in the visiting area, where drugs are handed over." This witness added, unsurprisingly, "If anyone talks, he puts his life in real danger."[240] This is on top of the substantial loss of "remuneration."

King Hoover's corruption appears to have reached even greater proportions. According to an informant: "When Mike Lane was director of the Illinois prison administration,[241] he'd often call in at Vienna[242] and walk a while in the courtyard with Hoover. Lane had had Hoover moved to the institution. Rumors said someone outside put an envelope containing cash into Lane's hands through some third parties. Whoever they were, they changed all the time, like they were some kind of circuit breaker."[243]

In a Nevada[244] high security prison, guards have been corrupted by members of the Aryan Warriors. Involved in drug trafficking inside the prison, these guards allowed gang members to use mobile phones to call outside. They also helped them pass messages between them. One of the opponents of the gang was killed after guards left the door of his cell open. Sixteen officers of the Nevada Prison Service (out of a total of 1,800) were specifically named by members of the gang at their trials.[245]

In Maryland, the police, the DEA and the prison authorities conducted an operation to dismantle organized trafficking in state prisons. Twenty four people were charged, mostly members of the Black Guerrilla Family, but also a number of prison staff.

---

[237] "I was paid to help inmates escape." Words of a guard in the *Cape Times*, April 1, 2004, 4. A former guard at Johannesburg Prison [Kgukutli Louis Pobe] told the Jali Commission how he and some of his colleagues collaborated to facilitate the escape of prisoners, how he was paid for this, and for remaining silent about complaints of theft.

[238] A fast food chain.

[239] Gear and Ngubeni. *Daai Ding*, 68.

[240] Tyson, Ann. "Prison Threat: Gangs Grab More Power." *The Christian Science Monitor*, 89, 160, July 15, 1997, 44.

[241] Transferred to another, non-penitentiary branch of the administration in 1999.

[242] Vienna Correctional Center, Vienna, Illinois.

[243] Knox. *Gangster Disciples*.

[244] Ely State Prison, White Pine County.

[245] *Las Vegas Sun*, May 25, 2009.

The network was accused of introducing narcotics (heroin and ecstasy), weapons, mobile phones, tobacco and even champagne into several prisons in Maryland. Thirteen searches were conducted and seizures were made in sixteen cells in six different prisons. One former guard, another still working at the prison and a kitchen worker at the Metropolitan Transition Center in Baltimore were arrested along with another guard at the Maryland Correctional Institution in Jessup.[246]

In Brazil, escapes reached a peak in July 2001. One hundred and six prisoners escaped together from Carandiru prison in Sao Paulo, through a tunnel. It was the largest multiple escape ever recorded. But not all attempts succeed. On November 8, 2003, more than eighty inmates trying to escape through tunnels, again in São Paulo, were greeted by police at the tunnel's exit—although they fared better than a number of their co-escapees who died of asphyxiation underground. In more spectacular style, some breakouts involve armed attacks, inside the prison or on prisoner convoys.

A survey of these escapes has shown that they were organized and funded by prison gangs, particularly the PCC. An escape attempt typically costs between 4000 and 8000 dollars per person, most of which is used to bribe the guards.

Escapes are also used to strengthen the organization. According to recent information from the Paraguayan police, an upsurge in robberies of cash transportation trucks, banks, and ATMs in the East of the country is attributable to a gang largely made up of Brazilian PCC members.[247]

In June 2014, eleven members of the gang escaped from the Brazilian Foz de Iguaçu prison. In another escape from the same prison, four months later seven PCC members got away to Paraguay. All eighteen criminals are thought to have joined the Paraguayan gang of Amado Ramon Benitez, a specialist in armed robberies.

B - Outside

Prison gangs are born and proliferate in prison, but their criminal activities do not stop at the prison walls. Just as contacts are needed outside to bring the objects of trafficking in, in many countries, "business" in the free world is managed by bosses in prison.

1 - The Management of Criminal Business from Inside Prison

Management of criminal activity in the outside world relies on communications. While the mobile phone is today undeniably the most practical means of achieving this, and while its use is growing everywhere, possession is not always easy to hide. The authorities are increasingly vigilant, and techniques for scrambling signals over a limited area are being developed, although they are not always appreciated, nor easily implemented.

---

[246] US Department of Justice, April 16, 2009.

[247] ABC Color, Paraguay. April 12, 2015.

According to legislation and the level of security of the institution, inmates may have access to traditional telephones or even computers, or they may resort to primitive communication methods, which are often very effective.

While it may seem extraordinary, the external activities of prison gangs are often carried out from those prison areas in which isolation is the strictest. Prisoners in these zones run no or virtually no risk. "Thanks to a secure environment, they no longer have to worry about being stabbed or challenged by a fellow prisoner, but can manage to send orders to the outside world. Because their organization is so sophisticated, they know that if a subordinate outside fails to obey, another will eliminate him."[248]

"*Kites*,"[249] in the jargon of US prison gangs, or *wilas*[250] for their Hispanic counterparts, are handwritten messages, finely inscribed on tiny pieces of paper. Originally, they were folded to form a square or diamond shape, with a yarn tied to one corner, hence "kite." The yarn was a security measure for retrieving the message in case of emergency during its journey from cell to cell. This obsolete but efficient means of communication, was used by the leaders of Nuestra Familia imprisoned in the high security wing of Pelican Bay prison[251]—where each inmate is isolated—to carry out criminal operations throughout northern California.

Written in lower case, and usually encoded, wilas are still frequently used, as authentication of the originator is often a requirement in criminal affairs. Again, official visiting hours serve to channel these messages, which can also be concealed in complex drawings. According to Cory Godwin, already quoted above: "It is a mistake to think that just because someone is locked up, he finds himself isolated, cut off from the world. They go right on influencing events. It's only very recently the authorities realized that what was going on in prisons could affect what was happening outside and vice versa."[252]

Among the orders sent out by Nuestra Familia, were *contracts* on traitors or enemies, guidelines on how to collect dues from drug deals and retaliate against rival gangs. In a message intercepted by the police, one of the leaders of Nuestra Familia in Pelican Bay, Javier Zubiate, convicted of murder,[253] ordered one of the leaders of a Street Gang in East Bay[254] to kill an enemy in Sonoma County.[255] In another, he asked him to set up a new chapter of Nuestra Familia in Sonoma.[256]

---

[248] Joseph McGrath, Director of Pelican Bay prison, quoted by the Santa Rosa Press Democrat, April 21, 2001.

[249] Kite, named either after the bird of prey (*Milvus* family, *Accipitridae*) or the toy because a rope can be used to circulate the message.

[250] Spanish slang for *Aquila*, "eagle."

[251] Security Housing Unit (SHU)

[252] Cory Godwin in Danitz, *The Gangs Behind Bars*.

[253] Of Joseph Littlewolf Lincoln, in 1995.

[254] Southeast of San Francisco bay.

[255] Over sixty miles north of San Francisco bay.

[256] Santa Rosa Press Democrat, April 22, 2001.

"It's not easy, said the Director of Pelican Bay, Joseph McGrath,[257] to admit the intense level of communication between these notorious leaders and the outside—it's how they keep their criminal activities going." Difficult to accept, perhaps, yet the highest level of security technology was for a time being totally defeated by little pieces of paper... are we sure this isn't still the case?[258]

While the medium seems unsophisticated, these communications are highly effective. Sometimes the prisoner would write the message with his own urine on the back of an innocent document sent in the mail. The recipient could read the secret message by heating the paper—a well-known procedure. Inmates also use what they call "ghost writing" where a sharp object is used to write on the inside of a carefully unfolded envelope, made of kraft paper a little thicker than normal. If well done, the relief should not be detectable outside. The envelope is glued up again and used normally, and the recipient reveals the text by gently rubbing a pencil over it. The text code used by Nuestra Familia in Pelican Bay consisted of a dialect derived from Huazanguillo, the ancient Nahuatl Aztec language.

The investigation into the activities of Nuestra Familia leaders at Pelican Bay, named Operation Black Widow, lasted from 1997 to 2001, cost $5 million and mobilized (in the greatest secrecy), the FBI, the Department of Justice and several Northern California police departments. In total, twelve men and one woman were charged, and their networks, sophisticated and effective, were dismantled. Six of the leadership's members were in prison. The operation uncovered at least fifteen murders around Santa Rosa,[259] and gave some insight into the Nuestra Familia structure in Sonoma, and its layered associations with members out on parole and in subservient street gangs.

The Mexican Mafia controls most of the drug traffic in the Hispanic neighborhoods of East Los Angeles from within the prison system, but also through its links with the 18th Street gang. The "Merit" of this solid domination dates back to the 1970s and a guy named Joe *Pegleg* Morgan. At sixteen, he began his life as a gang member by receiving a sentence of forty years in prison for murder. Despite this serious handicap to his early career Morgan managed to succeed, through control of drug traffic in prison and the methodical use of violence, in acquiring such power over street crime that he became, in the second half of his life, one of the most charismatic leaders the Eme ever had... while he was still in prison[260].

---

[257] Santa Rosa Press Democrat, April 22, 2001

[258] While it was noted that a leader of the Bloods, incarcerated in a prison in New Jersey, had ordered the execution of a witness by means of an SMS, assassinations generally require explicit authentication of the order-giver. *Probers say Bloods Gang leader Ruling From Behind Bars*, nj.com, November 19, 2008.

[259] In California, north of San Francisco.

[260] *Pegleg* was detained in Corcoran State Prison (California); he died of liver cancer in November 1993.

The prison roots of the Tien Dao Man differentiate it from other triads in Taiwan—it is described as "mixed" by local experts[261] because, alongside its illegal casinos and prison trafficking, it also has legal activities in the outside world. Its situation is unique in its attempt to remain legal while being entirely founded on triad money. Profits from legal business are in their turn used to help the criminal group. This "legality" remains relative. One of the charges brought against the "spiritual leader" of the triad, the recently convicted former independent parliamentary representative Lo Fu-Chu was that of "misappropriation of funds."[262] He was sent to prison for four years. Does anyone truly expect his criminal activities to cease—much less his legal dealings?

In Britain, according to criminal intelligence services cited in a judgment of 2009,[263] the Gunn brothers, Colin and David, leaders of the Bestwood Cartel of Nottingham and both in prison, continued to lead their group and organize their trafficking from their cells. Colin logged onto his Facebook account daily, allowing him to communicate directly with hundreds of people. By January 29, 2010, he had 565 "friends," prisoners like him or members of his gang, signing his messages with the very martial motto of the gang: "Chin Up, Chest Out". Although their use is prohibited, he almost certainly had the use of a smartphone.

2 - Prison Gang Control over External Criminal Groups

That prison gang members are bound by a lifelong oath is a universal rule. When they are released, or escape, they are fully expected to remain loyal to the group, especially to members left behind in prison. They most often do so, while at the same time resuming their criminal activities.

Those who "betray" the gang after their release or escape know they will be caught by the "law inside" on the fateful day they find themselves back in the prison system, or perhaps even before.

It is this relentless logic that largely explains the domination of prison gangs over the criminal population of the street—groups and individuals alike. In prison, there is simply no escape from their punishment. The penalties applied by the prison gangs are far more summary than those of the judicial system, and betrayal is always punishable by death.

Since 1993 the Mexican Mafia has imposed a "tax" on all sales of drugs to Hispanic street gangs in Southern California, designed in principle to help the Sureños in prison, a logic common to all prison gangs. Some Maravilla[264] gangs, ostensibly under the authority of the Eme, have refused to pay the tax, considering themselves

---

[261] "In Taiwan, we divide criminal organizations into four types—temporary groups, local gangsters, local organizations and mixed groups The Tiendaomeng belongs to this category of mixed groups." Yang Tzu-ching, former officer of the criminal investigation bureau. *Taipei Times*, November 11, 2001.

[262] *Taipei Times*, September 26, 2003.

[263] Sunday Times, January 31, 2010.

[264] Generic name of Hispanic gangs in East LA.

under no obligation to share their deals with the Mexican Mafia. To maintain its authority in the street the Eme started circulating a regularly updated list of recalcitrant individuals, called the Green Light.[265]

Appearance on this list for non-payment of the tax amounts to a death sentence. The Eme has given all Hispanic gangs, without distinction, a green light; to carry out the sentence as soon as it recognizes any of the individuals concerned, despite the truce in force between the Hispanic gangs, imposed by this same Mexican Mafia.

It controls many Sureños gangs nonetheless. For example, the Azusa 13, based in Azusa, Los Angeles County, whose leader had been sentenced to death. Led by members of the Mexican Mafia[266] out on parole in the city, the Azusa 13 embarked on a sequence of violent actions between 1999 and 2004, including many homicides. It was mainly responsible for collecting the "taxes" from drug dealers operating in the area. According to the Police, the real boss giving the orders was Jack "*Jocko*" Padilla, a leader of the Mexican Mafia, imprisoned in a high security cell in California.[267] Another example is that of the Puente 13 gang of Los Angeles County. Rafael Munoz Gonzales, alias "Cisco," was arrested for trafficking methamphetamine, cocaine, marijuana and oxycodone[268] in Los Angeles, Seattle and in the states of Alaska, Arizona and North Carolina. Cisco is best known for being a renowned member of the Mexican Mafia. Released from prison in 2007, he immediately took control of the Puente 13 gang,[269] which nevertheless has only some twenty members. These two examples illustrate the exclusive hold which prison gangs have over street gangs, exercising direct control over them.

As the operating machinery of prison gangs is to be found in a closed and secured environment, it necessarily recruits and forms its personnel within the prison, from among prisoners. Upon their release, these new leaders take their gangs in hand using the same means and connections as the prison gangs themselves. The reverse also occurs when members of a gang naturally re-establish the gang structure within the prison compound.

When US authorities decided to fight this threat, they split the leaders up and sent them to different prisons... resulting in their rapid metastatic domination of most of the country's institutions! In this way the prison gangs have extended their influence over the majority of American gangs and even those of other countries.

---

[265] This practice of drawing up Most Wanted Lists like the FBI, seems common. Nuestra Familia regularly publishes the names of the ten individuals it most wants to eliminate. Killing one of them contributes to rapid promotion.
[266] Gabriel Downer Aguilar and Robert Thumper Ramirez.
[267] *Los Angeles Times*, March 26, 2008.
[268] Oxycodone or oxycodon: semi-synthetic opiate manufactured for nearly a century from thebaine, a component of opium. It was designed to relieve the pain of trauma in war. It is found in commercial products such as Supeudol, Oxy-IR and OxyContin in which the proportion of the active substance is even greater. Its misuse has been observed since the 1990s in the United States and Canada, where it is a major public health problem. Oxycodone dependence is extremely strong, comparable to heroin.
[269] Associated Press, March 14, 2008.

Today the Mexican Mafia, the archetype of a prison gang, is often seen as a gang in itself, thanks to its grip on street gangs in general and its national and even international influence.

A similar phenomenon can be observed elsewhere. When a new inmate arrives in prison, the first question is always "who are you?" In the prisons of South Africa, he answers that he is, for example, a "soldier" of the *Gazi* line of the 28s.[270]

A new trend was observed in the late 1980s. Some new arrivals were hesitant in their replies, their use of Sabela was questionable, and their knowledge of the Nongozola myth was approximate at best—all indicating they were not "true" 28s, and probably knew nothing about the organization.

The interrogation would continue as follows:

> - "Where did you become a 28?
> - Hawston - a small fishing village 100 km from Cape Town
> - But there is no prison in Hawston, said the *ndota* (prison gang member).
> - I was not recruited in prison, said the newcomer. I was recruited by the *Rooidakke*.[271] I was given a job to shoot someone. They said that to get into the Gazi line of the 28s, you have to shed blood. They said once I made the kill, I would be a 28."[272]

The *Ndota* was baffled. Nothing so incongruous had been heard before in a prison.

Why did the prison gangs begin to encroach on the street? There are several hypotheses. Since the 1970s, there have always been informal and casual relationships between prison gangs and street gangs. At that time, the latter extorted money from neighborhood stores in exchange for protection, creamed off part of the income from liquor stores, levied "transit" taxes on cabs crossing their territory, and mutilated anyone who dared to work without their permission.

The two largest street gangs in Cape Town were the Scorpions and the Born Free Kids. In prison, the Scorpions generally joined the 28s,[273] while the Born Free Kids joined the 26s.[274] This was nonetheless only a superficial relationship. The walls separating the prison from the streets were sacred, and it was inconceivable that the 26s or 28s would be acting on the outside. In the same way, the Sabela language makes no distinction between non-Number prison gangs (Big 5, Airforce etc.) and street gangs—they are all part of the "fourth camp"[275]; they do not exist, even their tattoos are called *vuil papiere*, "dirty paper."

---

[270] The "Gold Line". The 28s are subdivided into two parallel hierarchies, two "lines." The Gold Line is the "soldiers"—the men, and the Silver Line is the "*wyfies*"—the "women."

[271] Rooidakke —"Red Roofs." A street gang known to the late 80s and early 90s.

[272] Steinberg. *Nongoloza's Children*, 39–40.

[273] A Scorpion would be made to approach the 28 "to extract the venom from its tail."

[274] 277. The 26s and the Born Free Kids were chicos, "good looking, well dressed."

[275] See above.

This situation began to change in the late 1980s as the imagery and rituals of the prison appeared in the streets—vulgarized, fragmented, widely and rapidly adopted. By the early 1990s, street gangs began to use the prison as a metaphor to justify their relationship with their victims. While throughout most of the twentieth century prisoners had imagined their prisons like the vast plateaus of nineteenth century Natal,[276] young people from the townships saw their neighborhoods as prisons, each lot representing a kind of cell in which the streets gangs are the *ndotas* and the shopkeepers they extort are the *frans* who must "pay for the air they breathe" like the "*frans* behind bars."

Street gangs thus monopolized the prison universe—its metaphors, its nomenclature and its logic—and impregnated the ghettos with them. This was the consequence of recruitment by members after their release, at the end of their sentence.[277] Those recruiting outside nonetheless had held no high rank when in prison and therefore had no authority to initiate new members, especially not outside. For these reasons, external recruits were systematically beaten and isolated upon arrival in prison. Some time later, "external recruits" such as Jackie Lonti, leader of the *Americans*, became rich and powerful. The situation then changed, despite opposition from many former members of the Numbers referring contemptuously to the interpenetration between the street and prison as "those who brought the fourth camp inside the four corners."

In the late 1990s, two of the largest gangs, the *Firm* and the *Americans* had adopted the full ritual of the Number,[278] and by the early 2000s, the *Firm* even began to call itself the 28s. Their leaders called themselves "generals" and named their captains, sergeants and judges.

Relationships have become closer. A recent study revealed that today real leaders of the 28s manage the *Firm*, while members of the *Americans* have brought methaqualone[279] into prison with the help of the 26s. The prison gangs and the street gangs have unified their culture, one which glorifies the ideal of being a gang member, respected for the degree of one's violence and disregard for the law.[280] The constant turnaround of incarcerations and releases creates a flow which carries this culture,

---

[276] Joining the 28s was seen as "a Homeric journey through a forest wilderness."

[277] Steinberg tells that in 2002 in Mitchells Plains (a township of Cape Town) he met a recently joined member of a gang in his neighborhood, the Jolly Killers, previously unknown.
- "I had some questions for him and he agreed to answer, provided I pay a third party in advance. A week later, I called to find out how his research was going.
- I will not do it, he said. I'm a 26. My job is to steal.
- That's stupid, I replied, it wasn't difficult, and if you'd have done it you would have earned a lot more money. He laughed scornfully.
- You do not understand. I'm a 26. It's my duty.
- Who made you a 26? I asked.
- The leader of the Jolly Killers went to prison. He became a 26, he said. When he came out, he made us all 26s." Steinberg. *Nongoloza's Children.*

[278] The "Americans" adopted the rituals of the 26s and the Firm, those of the 28s.

[279] Joseph, Norman. "Gang Boss Gets Triple Life for Naughty Murders." *Cape Argus*, March 25, 2003, 7.

[280] Department of Community Safety, *Provincial Gang Strategy*, April 2003, 3.

especially the myths of the Number, inside and outside of prisons. Associations of gangs formed outside persist inside and vice versa.

This osmosis between the prison and the street is well illustrated by the Smotriachtchii[281] in Russia who, still today and even when free, ensure that the customary rules of the prison still govern the parallel economy and the relationships between criminal groups.

A MENACE TO SOCIETY

The few examples we have been able to give and many more besides, along with the analysis we have made of them, reveal the gravity of the problem of prison gangs: Trafficking, corruption, extreme violence, escapes, and osmosis between criminal groups in and out of prisons, often replacing legitimate authorities, all demonstrate little-known and inadmissible flaws in the prison system as we understand it in states under the rule of law.

Prisoners have rights. This is the contract with those constrained to serve a custodial sentence. Yet these rights are systematically violated by prison gangs, in some cases to the ultimate extent, where the prisoner's life is forfeit. This is probably the most alarming aspect of the existence of these organizations, and the most inexcusable fault of those who remain silent or who tolerate their existence.

When a prison gang controls a prison from inside; when it is free to manage its "business" inside; when it tortures or executes other detainees; when the prison becomes a "criminal University" for any gangster desirous of education, promotion and prestige... just what role is this prison actually playing in society?

Today, we see in most countries around the world that even where the freedom of prisoners to come and go is strictly curtailed, their destructive influence is scarcely, if at all, affected.

Careful observation of prison gangs in many of the world's prison systems reveals a universal capacity to work around the constraints of imprisonment and to overcome isolation. They all yield profits enabling them to corrupt whomever they see fit; they will not hesitate to intimidate prisoners and prison staff alike, nor to eliminate those who oppose them.

In the final analysis they murder with impunity. The dominant logic of repression, in states considering themselves to be under the rule of law, is based on a criminal philosophy best qualified as autistic, tirelessly recycling gang members to the world they engulf and destroy, which endlessly regenerates them anew.

Although an emergent criminal phenomenon, prison gangs threaten the foundations of life in society. The question that must be faced is whether they are the only ones who stand guilty of this state of affairs?

---

[281] Literally, "one who watches", who plays the role of judge, treasurer, mediator etc.

References

Arendse, B. *Working with gangs*. Kinderversorger, Volume 9

Baird, L.H., "Prison Gangs: Texas." *Corrections Today*, July 1986.

Bartollas, Clemens. "The Prison: Disorder Personified." In *Are Prisons any better: Twenty Years of Correctional Reform*, eds. Murphy, John W. and Jack E. Dison, 1, 11–22. Newbury Park, CA: Sage Criminal Justice System Annuals, 1990.

Behan, Tom. *"See Naples and die" The Camorra and organized crime*. London, New York: I.B. Tauris Books, 2002.

Buentello, Salvador, Robert S. Fong and Ronald E. Vogel. "Prison Gang Development: A Theoretical Model." *The Prison Journal*, fall/winter 1991.

Carlie, Mike, *Into the Abyss*. Published on the Internet, 2002.

Commission of Inquiry into Alleged Incidents of Corruption, Maladministration, Violence or Intimidation in the Department of Correctional Services Appointed by Order of the President of the Republic of South Africa in Terms of Proclamation No. 135 of 2001, as Amended [the "Jali" Commission Report]. South Africa Prisons Ministry, November 2006.

Conrad, John P. "Who's in Charge? The Control of Gang Violence in California Prisons." In *Correctional Facility Planning*, eds. Robert Montilla and Nora Marlow. 135–147. Lexington, MA: Lexington Books, 1979.

Cox, V. "Prison Gangs - Inmates Battle for Control." *Corrections Compendium*, April 1986.

Earley, Pete. *The Hot House: Life Inside Leavenworth Prison*. New York: Bantam, 1992.

Enriquez, Rene "Boxer." *The Black Hand*. New York: Harper & Collins, 2008.

Farrington, Karen. *Maximum Security*. Edison, NJ: Chartwell Books, 2008.

Finckenauer, James O. and Elin J. Waring. *Russian Mafia in America*. Boston: Northeastern University Press, 1998.

Fong, Robert S. "The Organizational Structure of Prison Gangs: A Texas Case Study." *Federal Probation*, 54, 1 (1990), 36–43.

Freedom of Information and Privacy Act. Subject: Aryan Brotherhood. File Number: 183-7396, Part 1 of 1. Federal Bureau of Investigation.

Gang Beat. *Prison Gangs*. Volume 12, 4. Summer 2001.

Gangland Behind Bars: How and Why Organized Criminal Street Gangs Thrive in New Jersey's Prisons and What Can be Done About it. State of New Jersey Commission of Investigation, May 2009.

Gangs Infiltrating Law Enforcement and Correctional Agencies. Intelligence Report, National Gang Intelligence Center, January 15, 2010.

Gastrow, Peter. *Organised crime in South Africa: an assessment of its nature and origins*. Braamfontein, Republic of South Africa: Institute for Security Studies, 1998.

Gear, Sasha and Kindiza Ngubeni. *Daai Ding: Sex, Sexual Violence and Coercion in Men's Prisons*. Research report written for the Centre for the Study of Violence and Reconciliation, September 2002.

Gilinski, Iakov and Iakov Kostioukovski. "Le crime organisé en Russie, nouvelles approches." *Cultures et conflits*, 42, fall 2001.

Harland, Alan T. "Prison Gangs: Introductory Overview." *The Prison Journal*, fall/winter 1991.

Haysom, Nicholas. *Towards an Understanding of Prison Gangs*. Cape Town, Republic of South Africa: Criminology Institute, South Africa University, 1981.

Huma, H. *Prison: it is becoming a gangster's paradise*. Lahore, Pakistan: Nexus, 1999.

Hunt, Geoffrey, Stephanie Riegel, Tomas Morales and Dan Waldorf. *Keep the Peace Out of Prisons: Prison Gangs, an Alternative Perspective*. San Francisco, California: Institute for Scientific Analysis, Home Boy Study, 1992.

Hunt, Geoffrey, Stephanie Riegel, Tomas Morales and Dan Waldorf. *Changes in Prison Culture: Prison Gangs and the Case of the Pepsi Generation*. San Francisco, California: Institute for Scientific Analysis, Home Boy Study, 1993.

Knox, George W. "Gangs and Social Justice Issues." In *Prison Conditions and Prison Overcrowding*, ed. Sloan T. Letman, 1–19. Dubuque, Indiana: Kendall/Hunt Publishing Co., 1991.

Knox, George W. “Gang Organization in a Large Urban Jail.” *American Jails*, (January/February 1993), 45–48.

Knox, George W. *An Introduction to Gangs*. Lima, OH: Wyndham Hall Press, 1995.

Knox, George W. “A National Assessment of Gangs and Security Threat Groups (STGs) in Adult Correctional Institutions: Results of the 1999 Adult Corrections Survey.” *Journal of Gang Research* 7, 3 (2000), 1–4.

Knox, George W. *Gang profile: The Latin Kings*. Peotone, IL: National Gang Crime Research Center, (Published on the Internet), 2000.

Knox, George W. *The Gangster Disciples: a gang profile*. Peotone, IL: National Gang Crime Research Center, (Published on the Internet), 2000.

Knox, George W. and Edward D. Tromanhauser. “Gangs and Their Control in Adult Correctional Institutions”, The Prison Journal, 71, 2 (1991) 15–22.

Knox, George W. and Edward D. Tromanhauser. “Gang Members as a Distinct Health Risk Group in Juvenile Correctional Facilities”, The Prison Journal, 71, 2 (1991), 61–66.

Knox, George W. and Edward D. Tromanhauser. “Gang Training in Adult Correctional Institutions: A Function of Intensity, Duration and Impact of the Gang Problem.” *Journal of Correctional Training*, 1993.

Krajick, K. “The Menace of Supergangs.” *Corrections Magazine*, June 1990, 11–14.

Lane, Michael, “Inmate Gangs.” *Corrections Today*, June 1989, 126–128.

Lötter, Johann Morgendahl. “Prison Gangs in South Africa: A Description.” *The South African Journal of Sociology*, 19, 2 (1988), 67–75.

MacLennan, Ben. “Slow Puncture; Death Sentence for Prisoners.” November 20, 2002 (http://www.iol.co.za/news/south-africa/slow-puncture-death-sentences-for-prisoners-1.24444)

“Manual for visitors to independent prisons.” (Section 85-1 Correctional Services Act 111 of 1998, 1998), Office of the Judge-Inspector, Judicial Inspectorate of Prisons in South Africa.

National Gang Threat Assessment, National Drug Intelligence Center, U.S. Department of Justice, January 2009.

Nicaso, Antonio. Part 12 of a special series in the *Corriere Canadese* of Toronto, June 24, 2001.

Oleinik, Anton. "Un double monstrueux : la culture criminelle en Russie postsoviétique." *Cultures et Conflits*, 42, (fall, 2001).

Painter-Morland, Mollie. *Final Consolidated Report - Focused Assessment of Anti-Corruption Capacity within the Department of Correctional Services*. Pretoria, Republic of South Africa: United Nations Office on Drugs and Crime, 2004.

Pelz, Mary E. (Beth), James W. Marquart and Terry C. Pelz. "Right Wing Extremism in the Texas Prisons: The Rise and Fall of the Aryan Brotherhood of Texas." *Prison Journal* 71, 2 (1991), 23–37.

Ralph, Paige H., James W. Marquart and Ben M. Crouch. "Prisoner Gangs in Texas." Annual Meeting of the American Society of Criminology, Baltimore, MD, 1990.

Ralph, Paige H. and James W. Marquart. "Gang Violence in Texas Prisons." Prison Journal, 71, 2 (1991), 38-49.

Serio, Joseph D. and Vyacheslav Razinkin. 1995. "Thieves Professing the Code: The Traditional Role of Vory v Zakone in Russia's Criminal World and Adaptations to a New Social Reality." *Journal of Low Intensity Conflict and Law Enforcement* 4,1 (1995), 72–88.

Shakur, Sanyika (alias Kody Scott). *Monster*. New York: Atlantic Monthly Press, 1993.

Shelden, Randall G. "A Comparison of Gang Members and Non-Gang Members in a Prison Setting." The Prison Journal 71, 2 (1991), 50–60.

Smedley, Henry. *My Life in Prison Gangs*. Denver, CO: Bible Advocate Press, 2000.

Sykes, Gresham M. *This Society of Captives, a Study of a Maximum Security Prison*. Princeton, NJ: Princeton University Press, 1958.

Varese, Federico. "The Society of the vory v zakone, 1930s–1950s." *Cahiers du Monde Russe*, (October-December 1998), 515–538.

Van Onselen, Charles. *Crime and Total Institutions in The Making of Modern South Africa: the Life of "Nongozola" Mathebula*. Workshop paper. Cape Town, Republic of South Africa: Cape Town University Institute of Criminology, 1985.

Van Onselen, Charles. "The Small Matter of a Horse. The Life of "Nongoloza" Mathébula, 1867–1948." Johannesburg, Republic of South Africa: Ravan Press, 1984.

News & Opinion. "Making Prisons Safe." *Albuquerque Weekly Alibi*, June 14, 1999.

Confronting Cybercrime through Criminology

Xavier Raufer[A]

As far as cybercrime is concerned, we are still on terra incognita, or nearly so. "*Hic sunt dracones*," is found cautiously inscribed on medieval maps that are supposed to depict the heart of Africa. "Digital dragons" are ever more abundant today. Faced with these challenges, in the as yet uncharted territory of cybercrime, the only way forward is to think as criminologists and no longer as technicians. Why?

Look! Open Your Eyes!

As of the beginning of 2015, Internet advertising in France (25 percent of the market) has now surpassed advertising in the press (24 percent). Today, there are close to 1.2 billion Facebook users on mobile devices—an increase of 74 percent since 2012.

Humanity is becoming more connected than ever—standardized, formatted, remote-controlled. This is taking place in the developed countries and in the megalopolises, on a planet where stability is being worn thin, giving way to dynamism. In this society of perpetual acceleration, the intoxication of speed is felt ever more strongly.

What snares lie in wait for us! Notwithstanding the fairy-tales propagated by the titans of the Net, technology is not neutral, and algorithms are subtly partial. And listen to what British sociologist Zygmunt Bauman tells us of these fabulous mutations: "Unlike solids, liquids cannot maintain their form when subjected to an external force, however light it might be. Links between particles are too weak to resist any pressure. For Bauman, this is precisely the characteristic of human relationships in a liquid society."[1]

And we speak of mastery? This is a loss of control. We shower praise on emancipatory high-tech inventions? Yet cyber-servitude continues to grow. Obviously, all of this is criminogenic: fragilization, disorganization, and loss of attention are a veritable bonanza for thieves and fraudsters. These are the intrinsic perils attendant upon the system itself. But there are also hardcore criminals, cyber-predators who do not act thoughtlessly or cynically—but for the quickest and most hefty possible profit.

---

[1] Translator's note: Adela Abella, "Psychoanalysts Facing New Technologies in a World of Liquid Modernity," in *Psychoanalysis Online 2: Impact of Technology on Development, Training, and Therapy*, ed. Jill Savege Scharff (London: Karnac, 2015), 70. See Z. Bauman, *Liquid Modernity* (Cambridge: Polity, 2000).

[2] Translator's note: This quotation was back-translated from the French version.

doi: 10.18278/ijc.3.2.4

As an example, let's look at one of the Russian-Ukrainian cyber-gangs, one among many in the ex-Eastern bloc, as described at the end of 2014 by Group-IB and Fox IT. Calling itself "Carberp" after the "Trojan Horse" software of the same name, and starting in early 2013, this cyber-gang infiltrated its targets' systems by way of malware-laced e-mails that appeared to come from so-called trusted partners (the Russian Central Bank and others), and then proceeded to plunder the targets' bank accounts. Now it also preys on the systems themselves, which are heavy and inert, myopic, and even blind; it also attacks the computers in ATM devices.

Since its creation, "Carberp" has plundered fifty banks and ATMs in Eastern Europe, looting 25 million dollars. Since summer 2014 the gang has become even bolder, attacking businesses and banks in Western Europe and the US, thanks to a new "malware" package called "Anunak," which brings together a dozen tools used to steal passwords, break codes, enable remote cyber-theft, and more. Finally, "Carberp" practices criminal insider trading by stealing sensitive information relating to the targeted companies, so as to exploit it on various financial markets and stock exchanges, as well as in other ways.

Silent and invisible, great wild beasts like "Carberp" prowl a cyber-jungle where humans have so far struggled to deal with them. There is a bright future ahead for cybercrime. And what can mere technology do when faced with such beasts? Not a lot. We saw this recently when pirates ravaged the digital systems of the television channel TV5Monde, with all of the channel's anti-piracy IT staff entirely unable to see or do anything.

Confronted with this cybercrime, still barely understood, and now capable of striking whenever it pleases, as it pleases, cyber-criminology must prevail. A new criminology, one dedicated to mobility. A cyber-criminology forsaking the stable and the fixed in favor of fluxes and networks. A cyber-criminology of movement and motion, at ease swimming in Bauman's famous "liquid modernity." A cyber-criminology dedicated to understanding better, learning more about, and facing up to the emergent cyber-dangers—and alone capable of doing so.

Cyber-Criminology: What Does it Mean, and What Can it Do?

The objective of cyber-criminology is to tell us what criminals do in the cyberworld; here are its four foundational theses:

• *Diagnosis 1*: In the compound term "cybercrime," "crime" is dominant. Analyzing the world of cybercrime reveals that it has not invented anything new. In their own milieu, up to the present, cybercriminals have merely reproduced variants of physical criminality.

• *Diagnosis 2*: Cybercrime will not decline as a result of yet more advanced technology, but only through political will. An all-guns-blazing-style, headlong charge would provoke, in this domain, a disaster analogous to that of the inept high-tech war in Iraq.

• *Treatment 1*: What the cyberworld needs is a highway code—just as the society of the automobile, in its time, gave rise to its own. This code must be developed and enforced by a coalition of powerful nations, in the reasonable hope that it will be enforced worldwide. Another possible image for this indispensable normative superstructure would be that of the control tower.

• *Treatment 2*: The Highway Code applies to every vehicle, be it a luxury model or a more modest car. Similarly, only a code of the cyberworld would effectively penalize the predators, financial raiders, giants of the net, and others who plunder it with impunity and exploit its users.

An Agile Worldwide Digital Infrastructure? No, a Fragile One.

Today, the global system of automated data-processing constitutes a worldwide superstructure. Cyberspace represents a new continent, a new world. And these new information and communication technologies (ICT) alter the way in which populations think, believe, behave, and learn.

This applies to the whole population: honest folk, but also wrongdoers. Now, as always, when humans conquer a new area, it is not long before we see theft, fraud, crime, propagandist activities, fakery, and lies, among other forms of deviance from social norms. Cybercrime does indeed exist, and therefore cybercriminals also: in 2013, Interpol found that, on a global scale, more than 80 percent of online criminality can be attributed to transnational criminal groups. Today, this cybercrime is the Holy Grail for every felon. Consider the following:

- A total dissociation of time and distance, offering the ability to commit a crime at a distance of 10,000 kilometers (cyber-theft).

- Youth that are hypnotized, easy to dupe and infiltrate, in so far as they see "the world as a set of applications, and their own world as a series of applications—sometimes even as one single application, extending from cradle to grave."

- Cybercriminal masterminds, gang chiefs, or network bosses with almost guaranteed impunity—today only peripheral stooges are arrested.

- Limited costs for considerable gains.

- A simple methodology, exploiting two fundamental factors: human weakness (such as naivety) and technical vulnerabilities (such as flaws open to exploits)

Ultimately, in the ambient Internet world, we hear nothing regarding crime. Sometimes we speak of the effects of crime (attacks, intrusions. . .), but never, or almost never, of flesh-and-blood criminals—who they are and where they really come from. This is a dramatic omission. For if one thing is obvious, it is the need to start out by naming that which one wishes to understand, and subsequently deal with. Thus the discreet power of nomination is a formidable one: "Naming enables us to know. . . Naming unveils. . . By virtue of exhibiting, names attest to their magisterial sovereignty over things,"[2] as Martin Heidegger said.

In medicine, for example, failing to name a serious illness condemns the patient: in strategy, likewise, failing to give a precise name to a threat most often condemns the victim.

Cybercrime, Cyberterrorism: The Three Big Questions

Is cybercrime more dangerous than terrorism?

Quite recently James Comey, director of the FBI, declared: "The threat is so dire that cyber security . . . for the second consecutive year, surpass[es] both terrorism and espionage—even the threat posed by weapons of mass destruction."[3] Seriously? Let us understand the FBI director: he lives in a society formatted by, and intoxicated by, media hype. When speaking to the cream of Silicon Valley, any announcement that falls short of the first (digital) world war would inevitably trigger yawns of boredom.

Nevertheless, the threat of cybercrime is real. Today, the digital world is like the Bank of France minus the safety deposit boxes: generally, in most cases hackers of all stripes need only help themselves. In the past year, hackers were able to gain access to the systems of an American retail giant and steal almost all the confidential personal data of seventy million payment cards (those of its entire, massive customer base)—that is, a third of all cards currently in use in the US. Recently in France we saw the hijacking of TV5Monde: for a period of hours, the wholesale capture of a huge television network, its servers and diffusion channels, its accounts on social networks, and other places—something that was, for France, as huge a "strategic shock" in the virtual world as last January's killings (at Charlie Hebdo and Hyper-Cacher) were in the physical world.

After the TV5 hijack: Is France well-protected?

France lacks any mechanism for the early detection of dangers and threats. All too often, our official services react to a drama that is already underway, a crime already

[3] Translator's note: James Comey, "The FBI and the Private Sector: Closing the Gap in Cyber-Security," address to the RSA Cyber Security Conference, February 26, 2014, accessed October 8, 2015, https://www.fbi.gov/news/speeches/the-fbi-and-the-private-sector-closing-the-gap-in-cyber-security.

[4] Translator's note : Xavier Raufer, *Cyber-criminologie* (Paris: CNRS, 2015).

committed, but do not operate—do not yet have the knowledge, and therefore cannot operate—in a preventative register. Yet there is no spontaneous generation in the strategic realm, no more than there is in biology. The preparations for a violent act like the attack on Charlie Hebdo (in the physical world) or that on TV5Monde (in the cyberworld) will necessarily leave traces; what are called weak signals or "deviations from the ambient background," analogous to what ancient Greek wisdom called "epiphanies."

These are what we need to detect before the drama unfolds. In the months preceding September 11, 2001, multiple warning signs were reported to the authorities. But these signs were not understood in time. Essentially, their meaning was only realized on September 12, when the catastrophe had already occurred. This is what must be avoided. In strategic terms, what we need to do is simply allow France to apply concretely the popular wisdom of the proverb: "Prevention is better than cure."

An overexcited media often speaks to us of "cyber-prediction": can we take this seriously?

There is a generational question here: those who govern know little of the cyberworld and the perils it contains. In particular, they are entirely ignorant of the pernicious ideology of Silicon Valley, a highly toxic cocktail of scientism (Max Planck: "only the measurable is real") and hyperliberalism (so-called "libertarianism") bordering on pure and simple anarchism. The dominant idea in the propaganda of this anarcho-capitalism is that only information technology can protect us from the perils of the world. Thus it is affirmed, with unprecedented force: "There is no Alternative (TINA)." And consequently—so Silicon Valley tells us—the future lies in prediction via information technology.

Now of course this is absurd, because true uncertainty can no more be modeled today than it could in Aristotle's time. Otherwise, everyone would win the lottery or at the racetrack. This is absurdity verging on intellectual fraud, peddled to dupes by the giants of Silicon Valley. I expose all of it in my book *Cyber-Criminologie*.[4] Read it, and see what you can learn!

Burglaries in France: An Exploratory Analysis of the Characteristics of Victims and their Environments

Vincent Delbecque[A] and Inès Bettaïeb[B]

A total of 4.8% of households in mainland France were victims of a burglary at their principal residence between 2005/2006 and 2012/2013.

Among all of these households and according to their sociodemographic characteristics, it is estimated that those least affected by these types of offenses were households made up principally of single people in a disadvantaged socioeconomic position (economically inactive or unemployed). About 4.5% of this group were victims of such offenses, compared with 5.3% of households made up of socioeconomically comfortable couples.

The proportion of victims is also linked to the household's type of accommodation. Only 4.2% of households identified as tenants of a small apartment reported having been victims. Conversely, 5.3% of homeowners (or mortgagors) of large detached houses have been victims of these types of offenses.

Finally, the proportion of victims varies depending on the type of neighborhood of residence. The highest proportions of victims were observed among residents of densely inhabited or residential zones in the suburbs, with 5.4% of such households having been victims of these offenses in contrast to 4.5% among households living in densely populated and multifamily environments in downtown areas, and 4.7% in rural or periurban, low-density areas composed of individual housing units.

***Keywords**: cycle, crime rates, security, homicides, organized crime, police, private security, corruption, social controls, cyclical theory.*

Introduction

Burglaries[1] are a form of attack that stimulates both public debate and criminology research. They provoke public debate because after a steady decline in France and in most developed countries since the 1990s, the number of burglaries increased significantly between 2008 and 2013. This increase led governments to implement special preventative and informational measures aimed at citizens. This was

[A] Deputy head of statistics, French National Supervisory Body on Crime and Punishment (Observatoire national de la délinquance et des réponses pénales (ONDRP))

[B] Researcher, ONDRP

[1] Burglaries is defined as forcible entry, unlawful entry where no force is used, and attempted forcible entry.

doi: 10.18278/ijc.3.2.5

the case in France,[2] and also in Switzerland, Great Britain, and Belgium. For security and prevention policies to be effective, it is necessary to bring all of the available information to the attention of public decision makers and citizens.

Criminology, meanwhile, has paid particular attention to this topic, aiming to describe and explain its workings through the development of various theories. Three main currents allow us to grasp this issue by means of general or individual approaches, focusing either on the perpetrator alone or on the relationship between the perpetrator, the victim, and the surrounding circumstances.

The phenomenon can be analyzed using a macro approach, according to which crime is to be explained on the basis of social disorganization (Shaw and McKay 1942), decreasing social control, and the inadequacy of institutional control.[3]

A more individual analysis of motivation can also be carried out on the basis of the concepts of control and opportunity. Rational-choice and opportunity theories (Cloward and Ohlin 1960) emphasize the cost-benefit calculations (the cost of the punishment against the benefits from the theft) carried out by the potential perpetrator on the one hand and the significance of the lack of surveillance for the opportunity represented by the theft on the other.

Routine activity theory offers a more comprehensive approach to crime and brings together a motivated perpetrator, a suitable target, and the absence or insufficiency of control (Cohen and Felson 1979).The importance attached to the victim and the situation opens up a rich seam of analytical possibilities in terms of victimology and prevention. Since the early 1980s, these theories have stimulated a major school of research, and in English-speaking countries and some European countries they have often been applied to the theme of burglaries, particularly as addressed on the basis of victimhood surveys (Tseloni, Wittebrood, and Pease 2004).

In France, however, this area remains little explored. Research on some aspects of burglary such as the circumstances (Rober, Zauberman, and Névanen 2011), security devices (Le Jeannic and Tournyol du Clos 2008), and the types of theft (Rizk 2010) has been produced based on the "Cadre de Vie et Sécurité" (Living Environment and Security (LES)) victimhood survey.

This study addresses the issue of burglaries from the point of view of the victim and of his or her environment by proposing a typology of households and a proportional measurement of victims of burglaries in France based on the LES survey. This work is therefore very much in line with routine activity theory, since it sheds light on the characteristics of potential victims (the suitable target) and their environments. This study is also significant at the national level, since it offers an analysis that complements the relevant French studies, which, to our knowledge, have only partially explored the victimological dimension of burglaries.

[2] The Ministry of the Interior launched a national plan to combat burglaries in September 2013 (see: http://www.interieur.gouv.fr/content/download/84436/618928/file/2013_plan_national_de_lutte_contre_les_cambriolages_et_les_vols_a_main_armee.pdf).

[3] See Hirshi and Gottfredson (2005) for a summary of the subject.

To this end, we offer a typological analysis of households in mainland France, of the accommodation in which they live, and of their environment based on data from the LES surveys conducted between 2007 and 2014. We will first present the data and the methodological considerations related to the creation of the typology. Secondly, we will present the groups identified by the typology and the proportions of victims of burglaries, attempted burglaries, and thefts without forced entry for each of the profiles identified. Finally, we will discuss the significance of these results for empirical knowledge and with respect to potential public security policies.

Methodology

Source Data

In order to produce this study, we drew on data from the Living Environment and Security survey compiled by the National Institute of Statistics and Economic Studies (Institut national de la statistique et des études économiques(INSEE)). This survey, which has been conducted since 2007, aims to record the crimes of which households and their members may have been victims in the two years prior to the survey. It focuses on burglary, thefts from or damage to vehicles or homes, thefts against persons, physical violence, and threats or verbal abuse, and it covers both crimes that were the subject of a complaint and those that were not. It also focuses on the views of individuals concerning their living environment and security. Between fifteen thousand and seventeen thousand households answer the questionnaires each year. The sample of respondents is then weighted so that it is representative of the entire population of mainland France.

In researching the subject under consideration here, we used data from surveys conducted between 2007 and 2014 with households in mainland France. In particular, we drew on responses to questions concerning burglaries, attempted burglaries, and thefts without forced entry at the principal residence. In this study, this group of offenses may, for simplicity's sake, be referred to using the term "burglary."

Over the course of these surveys, around 132,000 households were interviewed. This sample was then weighted to be representative of the twenty-eight million households in mainland France during the period covered by the surveys. It is estimated that 4.8% of households reported having been victims of burglary, attempted burglary, or theft without forced entry in their principal residence during the two years preceding the survey.

In addition to issues relating to offenses against households and individuals, the survey allows households and individuals to be described according to their sociodemographic characteristics, their accommodation, and their neighborhood of residence. These characteristics may be those of the household reference person, all of the household, the relevant accommodation, or the surrounding environment. The descriptions of these were given either by the person interviewed or by the interviewer when the survey was carried out.

We were therefore able to draw on a set of indicators bearing both on the victimhood reported by households and on the elements that facilitated the characterization of households, their occupants, and their living environment detailed in table 1 and in appendix A4.

Table 1: Summary of the characteristics of households, their accommodation, and their neighborhood.

	Characteristics of the household	Characteristics of the accommodation	Characteristics of the neighborhood
Variables	• Educational qualification of the reference person • Household income • Marital status • Type of household • Professions and socio-professional categories of the reference person • Employment status • Age of the reference person	• "Legal status" • Surface area • Presence of a watchperson • Number of security devices • Presence of a dog • Type of accommodation	• Centrality • Size of the urban area • Type of neighborhood • Sensitive Urban Zone (SUZ) • Knowledge of burglary

Source: *"Cadre de Vie et Sécurité" survey, INSEE-ONDRP*

Statistical Analysis

With regard to exploratory statistical analysis, taking household characteristics one by one allows the proportion of households corresponding to the values of each of the variables to be "measured." Although this "univariate" approach (a single variable studied at a time) provides very complete descriptive information, it has two main limitations.

The first limitation appears when there is a need to treat a large number of variables or characteristics. The completeness of the univariate analysis loses its significance in the face of the multiplicity of the results obtained, and the interpretation of these results loses clarity. In our case, we have available to us seventeen variables for a total of seventy values. The exploration of all of these variables individually would be tedious and would ultimately teach us little.

The second limitation is that univariate analysis does not allow for a description of the relationships that may exist between several characteristics. This task, however, is of particular interest because it allows associations between various factors to be established, and thus allows new information to be acquired. These associations can be determined two by two through bivariate analysis. But once again, the problem of the number of intersections between all of the characteristics and of the exploitation of these results in terms of usable information arises.

In order to overcome these limitations and offer an analysis of the characteristics of households that is both synthetic and informative, here we use multivariate analysis methods. These are used to synthesize the available information, thus making it simpler to read and interpret. This study makes use of two multivariate analysis approaches.

The first is multiple correspondence analysis (MCA), which is used to synthesize all of the relevant factors and values into two composite indicators. It provides a graphical approach that aims to represent variables in a diagram and to measure their "proximity" or "likeness." This technique is not intended to create a priori categories; nevertheless, the graphical representation provides an illustration of the groups created during the typology (see below).

The second is classification, which facilitates the creation of a typology of individuals in the statistical sense of the term (here, households), thus allowing them to be grouped into homogeneous sets according to certain characteristics.[4] We used these two techniques in a complementary manner and for exploratory purposes on profiles of households in mainland France, relying on the characteristics presented above.

The synthesis of information through MCA and the creation of a typology of households were subsequently used to estimate the rates and the differences in the rates of victimhood with regard to burglaries between different groups. As a result, it was possible measure the proportion of victims within each group and determine the profiles most at risk among the groups identified.

Results

Creation of the Typology

Here we jointly analyze the graphic results of the MCA and the creation of the typology resulting from the classification for each factor (sociodemographic, accommodation, neighborhood). It is worth recalling that MCA is not supposed to establish a priori groups, though the illustration that it offers is in line with the groups created by the classification. Readings of these results are therefore complementary.

The first MCA was carried out for households' socioeconomic conditions. Figure 1 allows the distance between the values of the characteristics to be visualized via a two-dimensional diagram,[5] and allows associations between them to be identified.

[4] Readers interested in a fuller introduction to these methods may wish to consult Dehon, Droesbeke, and Vermandele (2008) or Saporta (2006).

[5] Two "axes" were defined for each of the three MCAs. Each axis is a combination of all the factors of origin and each factor makes its own contribution in each axis. Thus, the position of a value in the diagram depends on its weight on the first axis and on the second axis. For example, the value "unemployed" has a high and positive weight on the vertical axis and a very low weight on the horizontal axis. The reading of the position of each value taken individually allows the axes to be characterized, and the joint reading of the values allows the link that may exist between them to be demonstrated. The values associated with the axes (dimensions) in the graphs represent the representational capacity of each axis in the total dispersion of the values. In the case of figure 1, the two axes used allow around 18% (10.67 + 7.45) of the total dispersion of the values to be explained.

The two main axes around which the values are divided show a gradual increase in terms of level of income and level of educational qualification in the vertical dimension and of family status and activity in the horizontal dimension.

The grouping of characteristics notably brings out, in the upper part of the graph, a set of factors which may represent single people who may or may not have children (single parent families, not in a couple) and who are young (15–24 years). In the lower-right part of the graph, there are values that characterize intermediate and higher occupational classes, the upper-middle and upper classes, and graduate couples and individuals. Between these two groups on the right-hand side of the chart there is a set of values for people in couples who are employed, belong to a class aged between 25 and 54, and who have an educational qualification equivalent to the baccalaureate, the professional aptitude certificate, or the occupational studies diploma. In the lower left-hand part of the graph it is possible to distinguish in particular households whose reference person is inactive or a farmer and aged 65 and over. Finally, in the upper-left part, there is a grouping of characteristics that describe households belonging to the lower-middle classes or classes of modest means. These households comprise single people whose reference person is employed in a clerical or manual position.

The results of the classification (table 2) bring out four groups of households based on sociodemographic characteristics. The group of economically active couples with middle and upper income levels (denoted as H1) represents 30% of the households studied according to the classification made. This group consists of households characterized by the values located in the lower-right portion of figure 1.[6]

The second group identified by the classification brings together households of mostly young, economically active couples who belong to the "middle class" in terms of income, employment, and educational-qualification level (H2). This category comprises 20% of households.

Students or young graduates, mainly in employment and with high incomes (denoted as H3) (see table 1 for a more detailed description), and economically inactive older people make up the third group of households. Out of all of the resident households, 20% are assigned to this group according to the classification produced.

Finally, the classification includes in a single category households made up of a single person, with or without children, and households on low incomes whose reference person is unemployed or not economically active. This group includes precarious but economically active households and households of retirees. These two types of households have been grouped together (H4) on the basis that they both have low incomes. This group is the largest in terms of size; it alone accounts for nearly a third of the households surveyed.

[6] See the Excel file in the appendix for the exact composition of the groups identified.

Figure 1: Sociodemographic characteristics of households

To view image, scan the QR code above, or go to:
http://www.ipsonet.org/publications/open-access/ijc/volume-3-number-2-fall-2015.

Source: *"Cadre de Vie et Sécurité" survey 2007-2014, Insee-ONDRP*

The graph resulting from the MCA carried out for the characteristics of households' accommodation is presented in figure 2. A smaller number of variables and values is used in this representation compared to the previous one, making it easier to interpret. The first group can be distinguished in the top right of the graph. It consists of accommodation with a surface area of less than 40 m^2, located in an apartment block of at least ten homes in which the occupants are private-sector tenants. In the lower-right part, the accommodation is characterized by the presence of a watchperson or concierge and two security devices. Moreover, these characteristics are also associated with accommodation in apartment blocks with over ten housing units and whose occupants are low-income-housing tenants.

In the left part (top and bottom), there is a grouping of owner-occupied households and those of mortgagors of individual houses or townhouses with a surface area greater than 70 m^2. With regard to security devices, this part of the chart includes both accommodation with no devices and accommodation with numerous devices (three or more).

The typology of households according to the characteristics of their accommodation led to a distinction between four classes of accommodation for residents of mainland France over the period 2007–2014.

As the MCA highlights, there are first of all small apartments whose occupants are tenants. These homes are mostly equipped with one or two safety devices and enjoy the presence of a watchperson (A1). A total of 34% of the households are grouped in this category of accommodation.

Figure 2: Characteristics of households' accommodation

To view image, scan the QR code above, or go to:
http://www.ipsonet.org/publications/open-access/ijc/volume-3-number-2-fall-2015.

Source: *"Cadre de Vie et Sécurité" survey 2007-2014, Insee-ONDRP*

A second category is made up of apartments and small individual houses whose occupants are tenants. This accommodation, which has a surface area of between 40 and 70 m^2, is generally not equipped with security devices (A2). This category comprises around 12% of households and is thus the smallest in terms of the total number of people it contains.

The third category is characterized by the frequent presence of townhouses whose occupants are mortgagors. This accommodation is not specifically characterized by the number of security devices, and its surface area is usually between 70 and 100 m^2 (A3). In total, 20% of all households are grouped in this category.

Large, detached houses constitute the last accommodation category. They are associated with the fairly frequent presence of a dog, and the occupants are mostly homeowners or mortgagors. In terms of security devices, both homes that have no devices and those that have many (three devices or more) are grouped together here. This group therefore does not in itself represent a single majority equipment level (A4). This type of accommodation accounts for 30% of the households interviewed during the survey and therefore constitutes the largest group by size.

Figure 3: Characteristics of households' neighborhoods

To view image, scan the QR code above, or go to:
http://www.ipsonet.org/publications/open-access/ijc/volume-3-number-2-fall-2015.

Source: *"Cadre de Vie et Sécurité" survey 2007-2014, Insee-ONDRP*

The third MCA was carried out on factors relating to households' neighborhoods. The two axes identified by the procedure present, in the vertical dimension, a distinction between downtown areas at the top, periurban and rural areas in the middle, and suburbs in the lower part. The horizontal dimension presents a distinction by urban area size and density (type of residential environment). Accordingly, in the top right we find households located in densely populated and central urban areas; in the lower-right part there are households located in outlying urban areas; and in the left side of the graph there are sparsely populated rural or periurban areas.

The results produced by the MCA bring to light the links that exist between the different characteristics according to large groups of factors and thus make it possible to identify large groups of households for each of the types of factors used. This approach provides a graphical representation that is useful as a means of visualizing these groups. Nevertheless, an exclusively graphical approach may appear arbitrary and lacking in justification with regard to establishing relevant groups. This study also adopts a second, numerical approach, which aims to create a typology of households based on their statistical "likeness."

The results of the classification presented below were obtained using the same data as was used for the MCAs. As a result, they can be interpreted in a complementary fashion. The types identified can be illustrated by the graphic results presented previously while also providing these with a statistical justification. Indeed, the classification methods not only allowed homogeneous groups to be identified, but also allowed the optimal number of groups to be determined by minimizing intragroup heterogeneity and maximizing heterogeneity between groups.[7]

The groups of neighborhoods were established using indicators on the size of the urban area, the degree of centrality, the type of residential environment, and the proximity to Sensitive Urban Zones (SUZ) of the place of residence of the household surveyed. An indicator of the households' knowledge of the existence of burglaries in the neighborhood was also integrated into these factors.

Based on all these characteristics, the classification offers a grouping of households according to three types of neighborhood or environment, which correspond to the groups identified visually on the basis of the results of the MCA.

The first neighborhood group is characterized by a mixed residential environment (apartment blocks and houses) located in a suburban area with a large population size. A total of 23% of the households that responded to the survey were classified in this group.

The second group is characterized by a rural or periurban situation located at a distance from a SUZ and made up of a sparsely populated residential environment and a small population size. Within this group, households tend to be aware of burglary in their circle. This category comprises about 44% of households and therefore contains the largest number of people.

Downtown areas, which consist of a dense residential environment within or close to a SUZ and which have a large population, constitute the third group. These neighborhoods are also characterized by respondents' low awareness of the existence of burglaries. The households included in this group represent just over a third of all households residing in mainland France (33%).

[7] See note 1.

Table 2: Description of the groups identified by the typology

Characteristics related to the...	Group	Name	Description	Proportion
Neighborhood	N1	Suburb, mixed residential environment	SUZ in the (distant) urban area; area of apartment blocks and houses; suburbs; more than 100,000 inhabitants; no special knowledge of burglaries	22.7
	N2	Rural/periurban, low-density residential environment	Rural or periurban; far away from SUZs; scattered houses or residential area of houses, fewer than 20,000 inhabitants; tendency to be aware of burglaries in the neighborhood	44.3
	N3	Downtown, densely populated residential environment	Neighborhood in or close to a SUZ; estate or area of apartment blocks; downtown; more than 20,000 inhabitants; little knowledge of burglaries	33.1
Accommodation	A1	Apartment, small surface area, protected	Presence of a watchperson; one or two security devices; no dog; apartment block; tenant; 25–70 m^2	33.9
	A2	Small individual house or apartment, not protected	No watchperson; no security device; individual house or apartment; tenant; 40–70 m^2	12.2
	A3	Townhouse with little protection	No watchperson; not particularly well secured; townhouse; homeowner or mortgagor; 70–100 m^2	20
	A4	Large detached house, no or many security features	No watchperson; equipped with few or many security devices; presence of a dog; individual house; homeowner or mortgagor; larger than 70 m^2	33.9
Household	H1	Couple; economically active; middle/upper income	Couple without children; married; graduate; intermediate or higher occupational classes; in employment; middle or upper incomes; 35–65 years old	29.9
	H2	Couple; economically active; low income	Couple with child; low level of education; tradesperson or manual or clerical worker; in active employment; lower-middle class or class of modest means; 25–44 years old	20.4
	H3	Single person; higher income; in active employment or economically inactive	Single person or single parent family; no professions and socioprofessional categories, intermediate or higher occupational classes; in active employment or economically inactive; upper-middle or upper class; 15–24 years old and 55 years plus	19.5
	H4	Single, elderly person, modest income	Single person or single parent family; low educational level; tradesperson or manual or clerical worker; unemployed or economically inactive; lower-middle class or class of modest means; older than 45	30.3

Source: *"Cadre de Vie et Sécurité" survey, 2007–2014*

Victimhood Rates by Group

The classifications produced allow different groups of households to be identified on the basis of their sociodemographic characteristics, as well as those of their accommodation and their neighborhood (tables 1 and 2). Thanks to this categorization, we are able to make an *ex post* estimate of the share of the victims within each of the groups while also verifying the significance of the differences in rates between the groups identified.

Figure 4: Types of households, and proportions and rates of victimhood

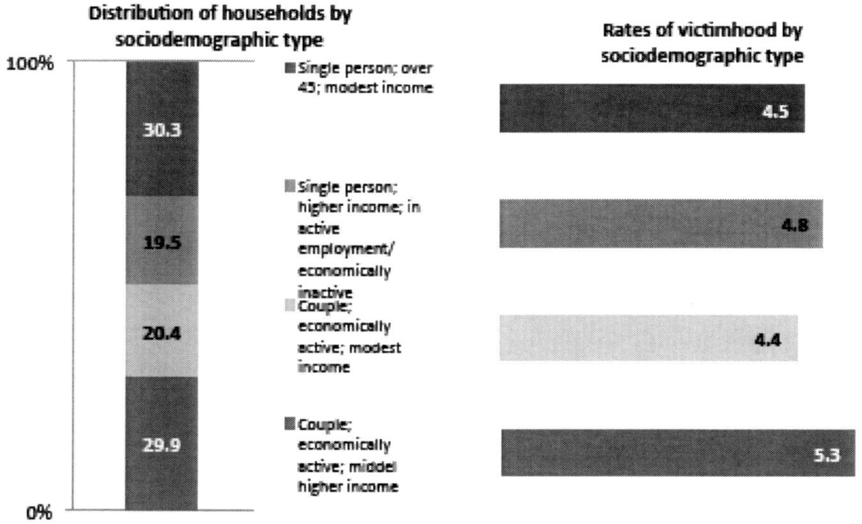

Source: *"Cadre de Vie et Sécurité" survey, 2007–2014, Insee-ONDRP, authors' calculations*
Field: *ordinary households, mainland France, rate of victimhood over two years*

The four groups of households identified on the basis of sociodemographic variables, rates of victimhood ranged from 4.4% to 5.3% (with an average rate of 4.8%) (figure 4). Within group H1, it is estimated that 5.3% of households reported themselves as victims. This is the highest rate among all of the four groups of households broken down by sociodemographic type. Over the same period, 4.4% of households in the H2 group reported having been victims of this type of offense. This was the lowest rate among all of the categories. Nevertheless, it is not significantly different from the rate for H4, in which 4.5% of respondents reported having been victims of burglary during the surveys conducted between 2007 and 2014. Among the households in group H3, 4.8% reported having been victims of the offense we are concerned with in this study.

The different rates of victimhood for these categories reveal that the factors of income and more broadly of belonging to a higher "social class" (higher-studies degree and high socio-professional category) are elements that are positively associated with the rate of victimhood. Conversely, households in precarious situations less frequently report having been victims of burglary than the other groups.

Based on accommodation characteristics, the classification has identified four groups of households. Among households in group A1, it is estimated that 4.2% reported having been victims of a burglary during the year preceding the survey. This was the lowest rate for all accommodation groups. For groups A2, A3, and A4, the proportions of households that reported having been victims of burglary, attempted burglary, or theft without forced entry during the two years preceding the survey are estimated, respectively, at 5.1%, 4.5%, and 5.3%. However, the differences between groups A1 and A2 on the one hand and A3 and A4 on the other are not statistically significant (see table A3 in the appendices).

The groupings produced bring out a distinction between apartments and other homes, as well as a graduation according to the accommodation's surface area. This typology is relatively faithfully illustrated by figure 2, which is based on the MCA for the accommodation variables. Victimhood rates appear significantly higher for individual and large accommodation than for multifamily housing. The characterization of groups in terms of number of security devices is made difficult by the simultaneous presence of non-equipped and highly equipped accommodation in group A4. As such, we cannot comment on the link between the number of devices and the rate of victimhood.

Figure 5: Types of accommodation, and proportions and rates of victimhood

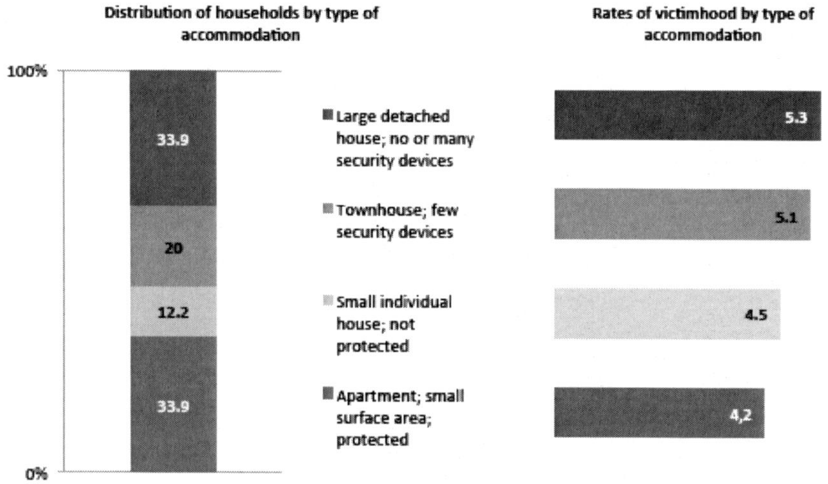

Source: *"Cadre de Vie et Sécurité" survey, 2007–2014,Insee-ONDRP, authors' calculations*
Field: *ordinary households, mainland France, rate of victimhood over two years*

Finally, the third classification provides a grouping of households according to three neighborhood categories detailed in table 2.

It is within the category N3—households living in a downtown area—that we find the lowest rate of victimhood. A total of 4.5% of these households reported that they had been victims. In group N2, 4.7% of households reported having been victims of burglary, attempted burglary, or thefts without forced entry in the course of the surveys conducted between 2007 and 2014. 5.4% of households in group N3 said that they had been victims; this rate is not significantly different from that of group N2.

A reading of these results suggests that it is the households that live in the suburbs and in densely populated areas that reported suffering the most burglaries. Conversely, it is estimated that households located downtown or in rural areas were victims less frequently than the others. Their rate of victimhood is, respectively, 0.9 and 0.7 percentage points lower than that of the households located in the suburbs.

Figure 6: Types of neighborhoods, and proportions and rates of victimhood

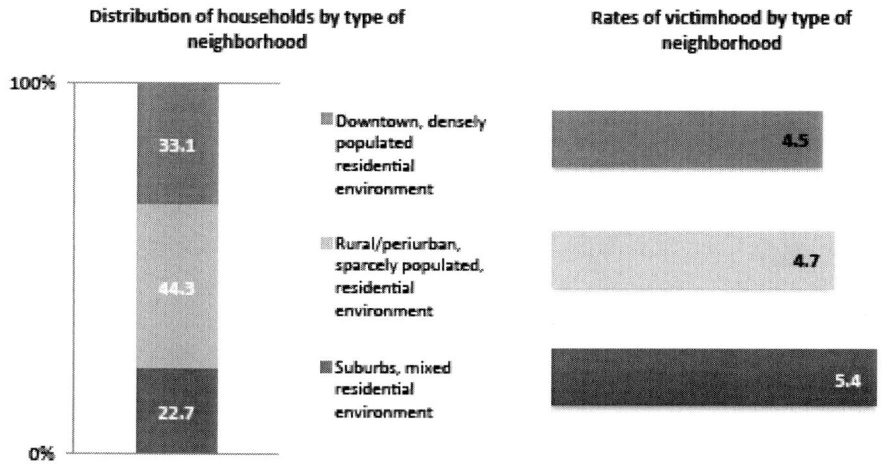

Source: *"Cadre de Vie et Sécurité" survey, 2007–2014, Insee-ONDRP, authors' calculations*
Field: *ordinary households, mainland France, rate of victimhood over two years*

Discussion

The results of the typology of households here provide some important initial information for the analysis of the characteristics of households in mainland France. On the basis of the characteristics related to households themselves, or to their accommodation or their neighborhood, homogeneous groups are revealed through statistical grouping. The groups identified in this way can then be analyzed in terms of victimhood linked to burglaries.

The decision to use a classification method for the factors used in this study seems relevant with regard to routine activity theory. The estimated rates for all the groups of households appear most of the time to be significantly different from each other, and taking into account the characteristics of the victims and their environment has a significant impact on the rates of victimhood.

Two main results emerge from this study. Firstly, with regard to burglaries, higher rates of victimhood are associated with households in higher social classes and with large, individual accommodation (two situations that may be complementary). In this regard, the "suitable target" highlighted in routine activity theory matches up here with a criterion of wealth. Secondly, the indicators related to neighborhood reveal a nonlinear link between the centrality of place of residence and the rate of victimization. Households located in low-density rural areas and those located in high-density downtown ones are less often victims than households in the peripheral suburban areas.

These initial results thus provide significant information with regard to public policy because they allow profiles of households that are more at risk of burglary to be highlighted. In consequence, the preventative measures that can be taken among the population can be adapted in light of these household characteristics.

This exploratory analysis needs to be expanded and completed, in particular by implementing analytical techniques to identify the effects of individual factors and by measuring their marginal effect on the likelihood of being a victim of this type of offense. In so doing, it would be possible to conduct more detailed analysis in terms of characteristics and to modulate the composition of the profiles of burglarized households.

Appendices

Click here to view Tables A1 through A4.

References

Cloward, Richard A., and Lloyd E. Ohlin. 1960. *Delinquency and Opportunity: A Theory of Delinquent Gangs*. New York: New York Free Press.

Cohen, Lawrence E., and Marcus Felson. 1979. "Social Change and Crime Rate Trends: A Routine Activity." *American Sociological Review* 44: 588-608.

Dehon, Catherine, Jean-Jacques Droesbeke, and Catherine Vermandele. 2008. *Eléments de statistiques*. Brussels: Ellipses.

Hirshi, Travis, and Michael Gottfredson. 2005. "Punishment of Children from the Perspective of Control Theory." In *Corporal Punishment of Children in Theoretical Perspective*, edited by Michael Donnely and Murray Straus. London: Yale University Press.

Le Jeannic, Thomas, and Lorraine Tournyol du Clos. 2008. "Protéger son logement contre le vol et contre ses peurs." INSEE.

Rizk, Cyril. 2010. "Les Caractéristiques des cambriolages de la résidence principale décrites par les ménages victimes." Grand Angle no.22, ONDRP.

Robert, Philippe, Renée Zauberman, and Sophie Névanen. 2011. "Cadre de vie et sécurité. Analyse des enquêtes pour 2005-2006 et 2006-2007." CESDIP.

Saporta, Gilbert. 2006. *Probabilités, analyse des données et statistique*. Paris: Technip.

Shaw, Clifford R., and Henry D McKay. 1942. *Juvenile Delinquency and Urban Areas*, 2nd ed.. Chicago: University of Chicago Press.

Tseloni, Andromachi, Karin Wittebrood, Graham Farrell, and Ken Pease. 2004. "Burglary Victimisation in England and Wales, the United States and the Netherlands: A Cross-National Comparative Test of Routine Activities and Lifestyle Theories." *British Journal of Criminology* 44 : 66-91.

Which Model for Twenty-First Century French Penal Procedure?

Frédéric Debove[A]

Introduction

Trying to adjust contemporary penal procedure to one unique model is a vast and perilous enterprise! A pessimist might add that it is impossible and unattainable, in so far as the current schema of our penal procedure is lacking in legibility, clarity, and predictability…not to mention intelligibility. An emblematic figure of the state's *imperium*, our penal procedure today is in migration, in search of a balance between pragmatism and ideology, a compromise between the imperious necessity of preserving public order and the no less fundamental necessity of guaranteeing the exercise of individual liberty. Vilified by certain intellectuals, destabilized when it malfunctions,[1] confronted with formidable new criminal challenges, goaded by the sensibilities of the moment, subject to crossfire between Europe (the European Council and the European Union) and the Constitution (especially with the new mechanism of the Priority Preliminary Rulings on Constitutionality [*Question Prioritaire de Constitutionnalité*]), and exposed to the legitimate grievances of victims, the French penal justice system hesitates between two paradigms which seem entirely opposed to each other: the inquisitorial and the accusatory—in other words, two emblematic figures of antagonistic models of justice.

This balancing act can be sensed right from the preliminary article of the Code of Penal Procedure that resulted from the law of June 15, 2000 (and was supplemented by the reforms resulting from laws no. 2011-392 of April 14, 2011 and no. 2013-711 of August 5, 2013). In stating the directive principles of the penal process, the preliminary article actually avoids making any commitment in regard to the old quarrel over which system—accusatory or inquisitorial—should be affiliated with our procedures. Far from being an inadvertent omission, this legislatorial silence corresponds to a voluntary and perhaps healthy renunciation of the opposition between accusatory and inquisitorial, an opposition that is oversimplifying in theory and which always requires further nuance when it comes into contact with judicial practice and contemporary situations.[2] A clarification is necessary here.

[A] Director of the Institut de droit et d'économie at the Université Panthéon-Assas, Associate Lecturer at ENM, ENSP, and EOGN

[1] See in particular the work of the parliamentary commission led by A. Vallini: *Au nom du people français. Juger après Outreau*, report 3125, tabled in the National Assembly on June 6, 2006.

[2] See in particular M. Langer, "The Long Shadow of the Adversarial and Inquisitorial Categories," in *The Oxford Handbook of Criminal Law*, ed. Markus D. Dubber and Tatjana Höernle (Oxford: Oxford University Press, 2014); A Garapon, *Bien Juger. Essai sur le ritual judiciaire* (Paris: O. Jacob, 1997); R. Colson and S. Field, "La fabrique des procédures pénales, Comparaison franco-anglaise des réformes de la justice répressive," *Revue de science criminelle* 2 (2010): 365.

doi: 10.18278/ijc.3.2.6

This distinction is above all of historical importance. From Greek antiquity up to the Middle Ages, the most widespread system in Europe was the accusatory system. From the eighth century (the time of the Crusades and the French Inquisition), the inquisitorial model progressively imposed itself, under the influence of the procedures initiated by the papacy and ecclesiastical justice: an expeditious, arbitrary procedure obsessively oriented toward the uncovering of crimes of treason against God (appeals for secret denunciations during preaching tours, anonymity of prosecution witnesses, dark dungeons, repeated torture to obtain confessions, burnings at the stake, etc.) At the time of the Inquisition, accusatorial (from the Latin *accusatio*: legal complaint) and inquisitorial (from the Latin *inquirere*: an inquiry into faith) procedures were not yet associated respectively with Anglo-Saxon and continental countries. It is only from the second half of the eighteenth century that these qualifications began to be used to refer respectively to the Anglo-American penal procedure and that of the Ancien Régime (the royal ordinances of Blois [1498], Villers-Cotterêts [1539], and Saint-Germain-en-Laye [1670] consecrating the dominance of the inquisitorial in French procedure).

Beyond its historical significance, the accusatory/inquisitorial distinction refers schematically to two antagonistic conceptions of the penal process, the first characterized by salient traits (public, oral, adversarial) radically opposed to those of the second (secret, written, non-adversarial). In practice, the "markers" of the two categories are far more numerous.[3] The accusatory/inquisitorial distinction is in fact a reflection of the sources of law (the abundance of jurisprudence in common law countries, rigorous codification in countries of the civil law tradition), the office of the judge (impartial arbiter or zealous inquisitor in an overseeing position), the relative position of the parties (egalitarian or nonegalitarian), the place of the jury and of professional magistrates, the system of proof (legal or moral), rights of defense (minimal or extensive), and indeed the existence of modes of recourse (more or less developed). The theoretical opposition between accusatory and inquisitorial procedures is also the result of different philosophies.[4]

Whereas the accusatory model considers as just that which has been debated and decided in an adversarial manner, the inquisitorial system puts forward a deeper and more substantive vision of justice, in reference to an ideal whose triumph must be ensured. Depending upon whether penal justice is expected to remain neutral (accusatory) or to be active (inquisitorial), it necessarily results in two different conceptions of truth: in the first case, a truth that is relative, and is the fruit of an equal confrontation between the parties; and in the second, an objective and absolute truth (whence the interest of certain studies on the relations between the different models

---

[3] D. Fairgrieve, H. Muir Watt, *Common law et tradition civiliste* (Paris: PUF, 2006).

[4] On this point, see P. Beliveau and J. Pradel, *La justice pénale dans les droits canadien et français* (Paris: Bruylant, second edition 2008); M. Delmas-Marty and J.R. Spencer, *European Criminal Procedures* (Cambridge University Press, 2002); M. Delmas-Marty, *Procedures pénales d'Europe* (Paris: PUF, 1995); J. Cedras, *La justice pénale aux Etats-Unis* (Paris: Economica-PUAM, 1990).

of procedure and judicial error).[5] According to certain authoritative writers, there is even a correlation between the different types of procedure and differing conceptions of the state—the inquisitorial system being affiliated with an authoritarian conception of the state, whereas the accusatory system is more associated with a democratic and popular conception.[6]

Even if the origins of our judicial systems go back to profoundly distinct historical and philosophical traditions, we should not allow the current opposition between Anglo-Saxon and continental models to devolve into caricature.[7] Congratulating itself on its presumed superiority as far as the rights of the defense are concerned, in practice the accusatory procedure is greatly idealized and overestimated: in point of fact, judicial error is a frequent occurrence in the US and the UK (see, for example, the cases of the so-called Guildford Four, the Birmingham Six, the Tottenham Three, the Taylor sisters, and those of Bridgewater and the Maguire Seven), and without the vigilant control of the Court of Strasbourg, the guarantee of the rights of the defense would largely beat a retreat: the equity of the procedure is regularly subject to manhandling by police practices that consist in violating the "disclosure of evidence" rule, and in not revealing to the defense the results of inquiries favorable to the defendant's case; the right not to self-incriminate is today weakened by the ability to draw negative conclusions from the silence of the accused. And finally, what value do the famous "right of silence" and "fairness of the trial" have in light of the secret detention locations where torture is used to extract confessions?

Inversely, sensitive to the sulfurous memories of its distant past (the repressive and purgative actions of the Grand Inquisitors such as Torquemada or indeed Simon de Montfort), the French model, imbued with the spirit of the inquisitorial, bolsters its respectability more each day by way of the right to a fair trial (Article 6 of the European Convention on Human Rights), which transcends all European justice systems and accelerates their increasing uniformity. Elusive, in so far as it surpasses the binary model (I), the originality of the contemporary French penal system lies in the hybrid model upon which it is articulated (II).

---

[5] On this point see D. Inchauspé, *L'erreur judiciaire* (Paris: PUF, 2010); A. Garapon and I. Papadopoulos, *Juger en Amérique et en France, Culture juridique française et common law* (Paris: Odile Jacob, 2003); C. Walker and K. Starmer, *Justice in Error* (London: Blackstone Press, 1993).

[6] Faustin Hélie, *Traité de l'instruction criminelle*, 1853; K.J.A. Mittermaier, *Das deutsche Strafverfahren*, 1832; Max Weber.

[7] See B. Danlos, "De quelques contre-vérités sur la jurisprudence de la CEDH en matière pénale," *AJ Pénal* 9 (2014): 404; P. Bonfils, "Faut-il changer notre procédure pénale ?," *Dalloz* 3 (2010): 158; N. Jörg, S. Field, and C. Brants, "Are Inquisitorial and Adversarial Systems Converging?" in *Criminal Justice in Europe. A Comparative Study*, ed. P. Fennell, C. Harding, N. Jörg, and B. Swart (Oxford: Oxford University Press, 1995); N. Dongois and B. Viredaz, "De l'américanisation des sciences pénales européennes," in *Mélanges offerts à Raymond Gassin. Sciences pénales & sciences criminologiques*, ed. R. Gassin (Paris: PUAM, 2007), 215–232; Colson and Field, "La fabrique de procédures pénales"; *Les systèmes comparés de justice pénale. De la diversité au rapprochement* (Toulouse: Nouvelles Études Pénales: Eres, 1998); *Un droit pénal postmoderne ? Mise en perspective des évolutions et ruptures contemporaines*, ed. M. Massé, J.-P. Jean, and A. Guidicelli (Paris: PUF, 2009); A. Bernardini, "Le droit pénal entre unification européenne et cultures nationales," in *Mélanges*, ed. J. Pradel (Paris: Cujas, 2006), 955.

I. An Elusive Penal Justice System: Beyond the Binary Model

The fruit of lengthy debates and of the lessons of experience, the French Code of Penal Procedure is traditionally described as the outcome of a compromise between two opposed models (like the prior 1808 Code of Criminal Procedure). Just as one might identify many architectural styles within one and the same building, each phase of the penal process responds to one or the other of these procedural models.

While the pre-sentencing phase (investigation and pre-trial) has historically been dominated by the inquisitorial, the sentencing phase is infused with the accusatory. Under the influence of factors as diverse as the European Law of Human Rights and the increasing sway held by transparency in the judicial sphere, the chronological caesura of the trial today finds itself carried away by overenthusiasm for the adversarial (A) and the dwindling of the secret (B).

A. Overenthusiasm for the Adversarial

A flag of pride for contemporary penal reforms, adversariality is without a doubt on the ascendant in our penal procedure.[8] The rise of this emblematic figure of the accusatory model impacts all phases of the judicial process, including that of the criminal court hearing, which is traditionally very close to that of a civil court (with the public prosecutor and the lawyers of the parties allowed to pose direct questions to the defendant or the accused, to the civil party, to witnesses, and to anyone called to the bar, as in the procedure of cross-examination so dear to common law). The progressive predominance of the accusatory is yet more perceptible in the sentencing phase, especially since the coming into force of the reforms resulting from laws no. 2000-516 of June 15, 2000 and no. 20004-204 of March 9, 2004 (in terms of the judicialization and jurisdictionalization of the application of sentences, as well as the organization of actual adversarial debates before the sentencing court). But this encroachment of the adversarial onto what had hitherto been the preserve of the inquisitorial is most noticeable in the investigation and pre-trial phase. As far as the investigation is concerned, the most obvious transformation concerns custody. Through the combined play of convictions under European and constitutional influences,[9] regulation of this police mechanism of constraint (especially as a result of laws no. 2011-392 of April 14, 2011 and no. 2014-535 of May 27, 2014) has now given way to a more adversarial approach, if only in the sense of the new role now played

[8] See F. Bussy, "L'attraction exercée par les principes directeurs du process civil sur la matière pénale," *Revue de science criminelle*, 2007, 39.

[9] Constitutional Council declaration no. 2010-14/22 QPC of July 30, 2010; declaration no. 2010-31 QPC of September 22, 2010; European Court of Human Rights, *Brusco vs France*, October 14, 2010; Criminal Court, October 19, 2010, appeal no.10-85.051, 10-82.306 and 10-82.902; Criminal Court, December 15, 2010, Plenary Assembly of the Court of Cassation, April 15, 2011, appeal no. 11-81.412, 10-88.293, 10-80.034 and 10-88.809.

in it by the lawyer (the right of the lawyer not only to conduct an interview with his or her client, but to assist the respondent in his or her hearings and interviews; the right to pose questions and to present written observations in regard to the custodial period; the right to consult certain parts of the investigation file). By a sort of capillary action, this assistance of the lawyer has even recently been extended to so-called "free hearings"[10] (Code of Penal Procedure, Article 61-1, in the draft resulting from the aforementioned law of May 27, 2014). As far as the pre-trial phase is concerned, the imprint of the adversarial so dear to the civil process is palpable in the progressive recognition (especially following the reforms initiated by laws no. 93-2 of January 4, 1993 and no. 2000-516 of June 15, 2000) of a sort of right of the parties to intervene in the course of the judicial gathering of information (the right to information, the right to contestation via requests for dismissal of a case, the right to direct the judicial investigation by requesting the carrying out of all procedures that seem necessary to reach the truth, the right to demand the presence of a lawyer during certain pre-trial procedures, and other rights.). In the pre-trial domain, we should emphasize, moreover, that the imprint of accusatory procedure has appeared as negative—or indeed, negatively—in the considerable growth of police prerogatives within the framework of common law investigations (both preliminary and *flagrante delicto*), and yet more so within the framework of investigations derogatory to common law (criminality and organized crime, terrorism, etc.). The more the police—under the control of the public prosecutor [*Parquet*]—are granted important prerogatives, the more the role of the judge—the emblematic figure of the inquisitorial procedure—is correspondingly marginalized.

B: The Dwindling of Secrecy

Even when it is not elevated into a directive principle of the penal process, as other rules inscribed in the preliminary article of the Code of Penal Procedure may be, the secrecy of the investigation and of the pre-trial phase is undoubtedly the "DNA" of the inquisitorial procedure. Inherited from the Ancien Régime, proclaimed by the criminal decrees of Blois, Villers-Cotterêt, and Saint-Germain-en-Laye, and reprised in article 11 of the Code of Penal Procedure (after having been abolished during the revolutionary period, with the law of September 16–29, 1791), the rule of secrecy is exceptionally long-lived. Yet as Alexis de Tocqueville observed, the rule may be rigid but the practice is malleable.[11] For, in the name of freedom of expression[12]

[10] Translator's note: *audition libre*—a new capacity granted to police to request a suspect's consent to an interview without charges and outside of police custody, and thus without any legal assistance.

[11] Alexis de Tocqueville. *The Old Regime and the French Revolution*. (New York: Anchor Books, 1955 [1856]).

[12] Articles 4 and 11 of the Declaration of the Rights of Man, Article 1 of the law of July 29, 1881, Article 19 of the International Covenant on Civil and Political Rights, Article 10 of the European Convention for the Protection of Human Rights and Fundamental Freedoms, Article 11 of the EU Charter of Fundamental Rights.

and of the public's right of access to information and ideas,[13] traditional and new media regularly end up interfering in the course of penal justice: sometimes by reporting the content of hearings underway as part of inquests or court cases, sometimes (better still!) by reproducing in full, and practically in real time, the minutes of a case filed in PDF format in the headlines of daily newspapers. The explosion of the information society—marked by the convergence of the printed press, audiovisual media, information technology, and telecommunications—is thus accompanied by numerous and patent abuses, and which go largely unpunished. The 1984 Gregory Affair (where the press was divided between those who believed in the guilt of the mother of the murdered child and those who insisted on the guilt of the stepbrother of the child's father), the Outreau Affair from 2001 onward, and, closer to us, the Clearstream Affair (with the reproduction of General Rondot's notes, the content of Dominique de Villepin's hearings, and even the minutes of the trial, including those of Judge Renaud Van Ruymbeke) and the Bettencourt Affair (with the resounding revelations of the online journal Médiapart, directed by Edwy Plenel) are emblematic of these out-of-control media affairs, which sometimes culminate in spectacular turnarounds (the media lynching of Judge Fabrice Burgaud after acquitting most of the defendants who had previously been qualified as "monsters"). Shot through by contradictions and a prey to cruel disillusionments, the secrecy of the inquest and of the pre-trial phase seem to belong to those mythical rules that are largely a matter of demagogic incantation alone, insofar as one cannot afford to gag the media.[14] Didn't Nicolas Sarkozy, then president of the Republic, declare, on this subject, that the secrecy of the investigation and the pre-trial phase "is a fable that no one believes in" (formal hearing of the re-entry of the Court of Cassation, January 7, 2009)?

II: An Original Model of Penal Justice: The Emergence of a Hybrid Model

Right at the heart of the paradigm of insecurity, attentive to the plight of victims, subject to onerous efficiency measures in a context of budgetary shortages,[15] prey to penal populism, shaken up by the exigencies of the European model of due process which can be traced back to Article 6 of the European Court of Human Rights (the "right to a fair trial," the standards of which are well known: the right to an independent, impartial court established by law; the right to be judged within a reasonable timespan; the right for a case to be heard equitably and publically; respect for the right to defense, and presumption of innocence), contemporary French penal justice has managed to develop original and hybrid traits. Although it indisputably scrambles the classical architecture of the French model (A), this singular development favors the rise of a new model founded upon compromise (B).

[13] An objective of constitutional status identified by the judges of rue Montpensier in their decision of October 10 and 11, 1984; Article 2 of the law of July 29, 1881 in the draft resulting from the law of January 4, 2010.

[14] For a recent illustration of this tendency, see European Court of Human Rights, February 24, 2015, *Haldimann and others vs. Suisse.*

[15] J.-P. Jean, "Politique criminelle et nouvelle économie du système pénal," *AJ Pénal* 2006: 473.

A: Compromising the Model

From the start of the new millennium and the solemn proclamation of the directive principles of the penal process within the preliminary article of the Code of Penal Procedure (on the model of those governing the Code of Civil Procedure), the route of our penal justice system has been traced out: it is that of the European model. Despite the constraints it imposes, this Strasbourgian compass does leave some latitude to French legislators. In the margins of the European (and constitutional) frameworks, the latter has been able to develop certain original rules whose effect is to reconfigure (or to disfigure, as the detractors of this movement would say) our procedures.

The duplication of the penal procedure—or if you prefer, the rise of an "encore" penal procedure[16]—is indisputably a primary source of imbalance. Thus, the fourth book of the Code of Penal Procedure contains thirty-three sections giving specific rules of procedure for particular offences (terrorism, criminality and organized crime, infractions of a sexual nature, procuring, drug trafficking, economic and financial offences, various types of pollution, and more). When the exception progressively tends to supplant the rule, the balance between the right to security and the right to safety becomes an exercise worthy of a contortionist acrobat. As with the "encore" penal procedure, the public prosecutor tends to become greedy, which is not without a certain danger for the separation of judicial functions. Although often leaving investigation for the investigative services to deal with,[17] the public prosecutor penetrates further every day into what used to be the "sanctuary" of magistrates—namely, the determination of sentences. With the development of accelerated and simplified procedures, and especially composite sentencing and appearance with prior recognition of guilt (CRPC),[18] public prosecutors—even though they are "neither judges nor magistrates authorized by law to exercise judiciary functions in the sense of Article 5 § 3 of the European Convention of Human Rights"[19]—accede to a new role which makes of them "an integral part of judgment." Once only the director of the investigation and the guarantor of discretionary prosecution, the public prosecutor now carries out quasi-jurisdictional tasks. This "professional mutation" inevitably confuses the distinction between sitting judges and public prosecutors, simultaneously eroding the sacrosanct separation of the powers of prosecution and judgment.[20]

---

[16] Following the expression ["*Bis*"] used by Christine Lazerges in "La dérive de la procédure pénale," *Revue de science criminelle* 2003: 644.

[17] D. Salas, *La volonté de punir, essai sur le populisme pénal* (Paris: Hachette Littératures, 2005), 159; J. Danet, "Le droit pénal et la procédure pénale sous le paradigme de l'insécurité." *Arch. Polit. Crim.* 2003, vol. 25: 52.

[18] Translator's note: *Comparution sur reconnaissance préalable de culpabilité*—court appearance with prior recognition of guilt, a kind of plea-bargain.

[19] European Court of Human Rights, *Medvedyev vs France*, July 10, 2008, and in the Grand Chamber March 29, 2010; and more recently and more categorically *Moulin vs. France*, November 23, 2010; *Vassis vs. France*, June 27, 2013; *Hassan vs. France*, December 4, 2014; *Ali Samatar vs. France*, December 4, 2014.

Taking a closer look, the imperialism of the public prosecutor resonates with that of the sentencing courts. When the role of Judge for the Application of Sentences was created (in the December 1958 Code of Penal Procedure), it was conceived as involving nothing more than the adjustment of the penalties pronounced by a court of judgment. The powers of such a judge were thus strictly circumscribed, so as to avoid too great an erosion of sentences. With the triumph of individualization, the determination of a sentence (particularly if it is a sentence that deprives one of liberty) has today been elevated into a privileged moment of personalization and of rehabilitation. No longer considering only the past, but also the future, the sentence is supposed to prevent recidivism by helping the convict find a normal place in society again. This perspective is considered so compelling that the courts for the enforcement of sentences are now endowed with prerogatives (Article 707 sq., and especially Article 714 sq., of the Code of Penal Procedure) which are liable to appreciably denature the punishment that is imposed, and with it the authority of the case being judged and the separation of the phases of judgment and sentencing.

B. The Model of Compromise

Insofar as it is closely linked to a dynamic of the "privatization" of the trial, the notion of contractualization may appear on first glance to be foreign to the inquisitorial procedure, of which the penal process still seems to be the emblematic figure.[21] However, as the sentencing system takes on the responsibility of suppressing any act that disturbs public order, the conflict between the two goes beyond the protagonists alone. Thus, the penal process accords a place to individual wills, whether that of the offender or that of the victim. Although this is nothing new, the contemporary development of this phenomenon is an expression of the rise of negotiated penal justice, along with the correlative retreat of a justice imposed from above.[22]

As the golden thread of the penal process, presented as a remedy for all the ills of the justice system, contractualization is certainly alluring. However, at the risk of slight exaggeration, when common law encounters penal justice, it leaves the latter intact and unchanged—like water off a duck's back. Why? Essentially because of contractual imbalance.

---

[20] See, among others, P. Maistre du Chambon, "Observations hétérodoxes sur quelques évolutions de la procédure pénale," in Pradel (ed.) *Mélanges*, 395; F. Molins, "Le procureur de la République, nouveau pivot de la justice pénale," in *Le nouveau processus pénal après la loi Perben II* (Paris: Dalloz, 2004), 365.
[21] X. Pin, "La privatisation du procès," *Revue de science criminelle* 2002: 245; Y. Benhamou, "Vers une inexorable privatisation de la justice," *Dalloz* 2003: Chron. 2771.
[22] On this point, see *Réforme de la justice, réforme de l'Etat*, ed. L. Cadiet and L. Richer (Paris: PUF, 2003); *Les modes alternatifs de règlement des litiges: les voies nouvelles d'une autre justice*, ed. P. Chevalier, Y. Desdevises and P. Milburn (Paris: La Documentation française, 2003); X. Lagarde, "Transaction et ordre public," *Dalloz* 2000: Chron. 217; C. Saas, "De la composition pénale au plaider-coupable: le pouvoir de sanction du procureur," *Revue de science criminelle* 2004: 827; M. Dobkine, "La transaction en matière pénale," *Dalloz* 1994: Chron. 137; C. Lazerges, "Médiation pénale, justice pénale et politique criminelle," Revue de science criminelle 1997: 186.

The various forms of negotiated justice (composite sentencing, appearance with prior recognition of guilt, etc.) do indeed seem very closely related to the notion of the contract. This proximity appeared first with the exchange of assent when an offer is made (whether at the trial, judgment, or sentencing stage) and accepted, sometimes tacitly, sometimes explicitly. Furthermore, as is the case for civil proceedings, penal law contains many precautions to make sure that the acceptance of such an offer by an offender—major and sometimes minor—is the act of an enlightened will: information as to the type of agreement being made and the resulting juridical consequences, as well as the establishment of a period for reflection and changing one's mind, are a part of this approach. The attraction of the contractual model goes further, with the reciprocal obligations that result from the meeting of minds: the offender obliges himself or herself to do or not to do certain things; as a counterpart, the judicial authority abstains from prosecuting, judging, or sanctioning him or her in peremptory manner. Finally, in the case that the offender-debtor does not carry out his or her obligations, or does so imperfectly, the contract of trust is dissolved and the sword of justice takes the place of the granting of damages.

Albeit seductive, this intellectual construction is rather artificial, for contractual justice is ideally characterized by a twofold balance—between the parties and their reciprocal obligations—that is largely foreign to the penal process.[23]

First of all, this imbalance is flagrant when the offer to contract an agreement is presented. At whatever stage of the penal process this occurs, the offender has no right to negotiate. It is "take it or leave it" (unlike the various American practices of negotiated justice, in which negotiation can bear upon the charges made against the accused—charge bargaining—or the penalty—sentence bargaining—or even on the judge by whom the case will be tried—"judge shopping"). The concession made by the judicial authority consists in permitting the offender to accept a proposition, without being able to make any counter-proposition in return. Any contract written in advance, any negotiations, discussions, and other bargaining are theoretically external to French penal law. Thus the public prosecutor is free to set the law in motion against any offender who declares that he has accepted in advance an alternative arrangement to legal proceedings. The contractualist vision of the penal process, already somewhat remodeled in regard to the contract offer, is further modified as far as the burden of risk in the case of a breakdown of negotiations is concerned.

No one who does not wish to enter into a contract shall do so—such is the principle of liberal-individualist civil law. Being free, an individual can refuse to enter into a contract with anyone who makes the offer to him or her. As a general rule, there is no gainsaying such a refusal, nor does it imply any further responsibility for the one who refuses. But the elective character of consent is not so rigorously protected in the constrained environment of the penal process. Certain defendants, although innocent, may be tempted to accept a proposition made to them with the sole aim of escaping

[23] On this point see B. Pereira, "Justice négociée: efficacité répressive et droits de la défense," *Dalloz* 2005: Chron. 2041.

penal proceedings or the uncertain prospect of a possible heavier sentence. This fear of judicial error, which vitiates consent, is a grave threat to innocent defendants, who are naturally more "risk-phobic" than defendants who are actually guilty.

On top of this fear of risk there is the "penal price" to be paid in case of a refusal to contract an agreement. Although in principle the defendant is free to refuse the proposition of the judicial authority, this freedom is chancy, temporary, and costly in terms of resources. Thus, one who refuses to assent to a search within the framework of a preliminary investigation risks being placed in custody (although in some circumstances this refusal may also be overcome by order of the liberties and detention judge). A defendant who refuses to come to court following a summons may be constrained to do so by use of force (Code of Penal Procedure, Article 78). Similarly, a defendant who refuses the composite sentence proposed by the public prosecutor opens himself up to the possibility that proceedings may be initiated against him or her (Code of Penal Procedure, Article 41-2). From the same perspective, a defendant who does not accept the sentence passed following an appearance with prior recognition of guilt is in principle sent back either before the instructing magistrate or before the Criminal Court, with all the uncertainties implied by such procedures (Code of Penal Procedure, Article 495-12). These ethically questionable retaliatory measures are present throughout the whole penal process, and in practice tend to pressurize the offender into capitulating, especially if he is short of money and cannot afford the services of a lawyer with irreproachable professional qualities throughout the trial proceedings.

Conclusion

Ultimately, contractualization is to the penal process what the contract of adhesion is to the theory of contracts. The strategic superiority of one of the parties, and the resulting absence of any power to negotiate, the unilateral—not to say one-sided—character of the clauses of the transaction, and the mass litigation which the approach intends to remedy, are so many sources of abuse. Furthermore, the risk of arbitrariness is accompanied by a possible departure from the principle of equality before the penal law, insofar as the content of the "contract" is not standardized, and varies appreciably depending upon the offender and the circumstances of the offence. It is understandable, under such conditions, that the shadow of the judge looms over the whole process, and especially in regard to the mechanisms of validation (composite sentencing) and qualification (appearance with prior admission of guilt).

Criminal–Terrorist Convergence: Intelligence Co-production for Transnational Threats*

John P. Sullivan

Contemporary nonstate threats including criminal cartels, gangs, mafias, insurgents, and terrorists operate on a global scope with distinct local characteristics. Local actors link with global actors to conduct operations through alliances and within a range of network configurations. The expanding reach of criminal, terrorist, and hybrid actors challenge local, national, and global security as crime and war converge. This paper will look into the types of connections among local–global actors and at the need for networked, global criminal, and security intelligence operations, including co-operative intelligence fusion (intelligence co-production) to address transnational crime and terrorism.

The convergence of nonstate threats poses a challenge to state response capacity. A range of nonstate threats states face. These include gangs, transnational organized crime (mafias and criminal cartels), and terrorists. Of course, each of these poses unique challenges in terms of their focus of operation, geographic reach, and level of sophistication. They also present a labyrinth of interconnected challenges as the individual groups form temporary and opportunistic connections. These connections may be short lived spanning a single transaction through longer-term alliances and at times joint ventures.

Threat Convergence

The complex, protean nature of criminal enterprises of all varieties makes assessing their capabilities a full-time, endeavor. The same holds true for terrorist groups.[1] Changes in strategic situation, competition for power and influence within the organization and among peer competitors makes the world of gangs and terrorists a volatile environment. The gangs, terrorist and insurgent groups, and cells are often in competition with themselves, competitors, and the various states they challenge. Often this competition is solved through violence. Assassinations, drive-by shootings, and brutal acts encompassing barbaric tactics such as beheadings and dismemberment are among the solutions chosen. Attacks against rivals, elements of the state, and civilians are also employed to shape the various groups market share and survival.

*From *ISA 2015 New Orleans, LA, February 18–21, 2015*. Panel on *Assessing Nonstate Threats: Global and Regional Perspectives on Terrorism and Transnational Crime.*

doi: 10.18278/ijc.3.2.7

Convergence of criminal, terrorist, and insurgent threat streams (and actors) is a study in illicit (and grey-area) networks and globalization. In fact, some view this as 'deviant globalization'[2] where illicit flows are taped to extract resources, wealth, and power.[3]

Defining the nature of convergence is as complex as the variety of groups involved. As a starting point, it is important to remember that all of the groups involved in this treat convergence are criminal organizations. It is their motivations (which shift with time, and are often mixed) that differentiate their specific niche. Gangs themselves include street and prison gangs (often interconnected) that can span several generations (or *loci*) of activity. Terrorists and insurgents are actively seeking political change but rely upon a range of criminal activities to sustain their activities. Mafias and cartels seek profit, but often use violence and attacks on the state to secure space and freedom to operate. And of course, some groups morph and change focus over time. Remember, Martin van Creveld (as I have often noted) said, "Future war will not be waged by armies but by groups whom today we call terrorists, guerillas, bandits, and robbers, but who will undoubtedly hit upon more formal titles to describe themselves."[4]

This essentially describes non-Trinitarian (van Creveld) or Fourth Generation Warfare (4GW)[5] where hybrid bands attack society and societal bonds to destroy political will. As Joseph Nye pointed out: "While particular generational delineations are somewhat arbitrary, they reflect an important trend: the blurring of the military front and the civilian rear. Accelerating this shift is the replacement of interstate war by armed conflict involving nonstate actors such as insurgent groups, terrorist networks, militias, and criminal organizations."[6]

Street gangs can be described as fitting into one of three generations: turf (1st gen); market (2nd gen); and mercenary/political (3rd gen).[7] To complicate this, gangs can be connected to other gangs and/or organized crime groups through franchise arrangements, alliances, and familial linkages among individual members. This makes power within the constellation of gangs subject to a set of complex networks of influence. Cartels can also evolve or fall into three phases: 1st phase cartel (aggressive competitor); 2nd phase cartel (subtle co-opter): and 3rd phase cartel (criminal state successor).[8] The third-phase cartel envisioned a state competitor of the type seen in Mexico's criminal insurgencies.[9] Both criminal insurgencies and the emergence of narco-enclaves[10] and criminalized (mafia) states involving hybrid criminal–terrorist–state franchises pose a significant national and global security threat.[11] Essentially this involves strategic crime.

Terrorists and insurgents, including *jihadi* networks, often rely upon crime to support their operations. Drug trafficking, robbery, extortion, and smuggling became potent revenue sources for terrorists and insurgents. This reliance on illicit revenue streams also brings the terrorist networks and its individual actors into contact with criminal gangs. New opportunities for revenue on both sides now exist to be exploited and they are. Understanding these linkages is a challenge for police, intelligence, and security scholars. (More on that later.)

Threat Actors

The hybrid actors involved in convergence include gangs, transnational organized crime (cartels, mafias), terrorists, and co-opted elements of various states.

Transnational gangs are one notable component in this mix. The most notable transnational gangs are the *maras*: Mara Salvatrucha 13 (MS-13) and Eighteenth Street (M-18) both originating in Los Angeles, but now operating throughout the United States and in Mexico and Central America (notably El Salvador and Honduras).[12] These transnational linkages are variable, subtle, but real, often the result of migration and/or deportation of gang's members rather than a deliberate business strategy. The connections include individuals, individual cliques (or sub-sets of the gang), and networks combining both. Much of the activity is self-initiated at all levels, but influence and varying degrees of control are concentrated at key hubs (e.g., Los Angeles, San Salvador). Rather than view the links between gang's hubs as a command and control relationship, it is useful to view it as "networks of influence."[13] Both MS-13 and M-18 owe fealty to *La Eme* (the Mexican Mafia) in Los Angeles and pay a street tax ("quota" to that prison gangs for activities in Eme's sphere of influence.[14] The *maras* have dominated local gangs or *pandillas* and have executed alliances with other entities such as drug cartels, notably an MS-13–Zetas alliance.[15]

Cross-border gangs are a variation of transnational gangs. A notable example is found in *Barrio Azteca* (BA) (known as *Los Aztecas* in Mexico) in the El Paso–Ciudad Juárez area.[16] BA is a combination of street–prison gangs with bi-national reach. BA was an integral component of *La Línea* an enforcement network for the Vicente Carillo Fuentes Organization (VCF/Juárez Cartel). *La Línea* is a specialized entity found in the Juárez *plaza*. It served to protect the VCF and is comprised of drug dealers, *sicarios* (hit men), and corrupt police officials. It is an adaptive, hybrid entity within the networked nonstate actors in Mexico's narco-conflict. As described by Sullivan and Logan:[17]

> Essentially, La Línea is a networked gang, a specialized node in a transnational criminal enterprise. It appears to be operating as more than a turf-oriented street gang (a first-generation gang) or even a narco-trafficking gang (a second-generation gang). It appears to act as a specialized variant of a third-generation gang essentially serving as mercenaries. It has transnational reach through its allies and inter-networked cross-border gangs and cartel partners. It demonstrates a higher degree of sophistication than many gangs, and it even fulfills para-political functions for its cartel employer. Its network configuration enables morphing form to exploit custom network links to carry out specific, specialized missions.
>
> The La Línea node is a hybrid entity, essentially a third-generation gang composed partially of corrupted law enforcement officers and serving as a bridge between street gangs and organized crime. Its structure consists of interlocking membership within

> allied organizations of nodes (much like elites who serve on multiple corporate boards).
>
> Here we see something similar to a feudal knight serving both his local liege (i.e., home gang) and a higher authority (i.e., the cartel). This neo-feudal organization of the parallel governance space, combined with its unbridled brutality/lethality and organizational flexibility, makes it a significant threat to public safety and an important case study in transitional criminal forms. In this case, it appears that La Línea is a violent nonstate actor operating as a private army.

Links between gangs and cartels are common. Recent estimates link 61 U.S. gangs with Mexican cartel activity (with 10 operating in the El Paso–Ciudad Juárez *plaza* alone.) in that plaza, the gangs include: *BA*, Latin Kings, and *La Hermandad de Pistoleros Latinos* (linked with the Juárez Cartel) and *Los Sureños*, Tango Blast, and Latin Kings (linked with the Sinaloa Federation). (The Latin Kings work for or with multiple cartels.)[18]

Transnational crime involves organized criminal enterprises that operate on a global scale.[19] These groups include the Sicilian Mafia, Neapolitan *Camorra*, Calabrian *'Ndrangheta*[20] as well as Mexican criminal cartels, and Asian triads. Dawood Ibrahim's D-Company is a notorious South Asia crime syndicate that has been linked to *jihadis* including the *Lashkar-e-Taiba* and *Boko Haram*.[21]

Terrorist and insurgents also engage in crime to support their primary goal, and some even transition into essentially criminal bands. The FARC (*Fuerzas Armadas Revolucionarias de Colombia* or Revolutionary Armed Forces of Colombia) started as a revolutionary group. It utilized drug trafficking, extortion, and kidnapping to support its operations to the degree that criminal enterprise largely supplanted political activism. The FARC maintained links with drug cartels, terrorists (including Hezbollah), and states (Venezuela). The Taliban in Afghanistan also relied upon narco-trafficking to sustain funding.[22] Drug trafficking is a key element of convergence.[23]

The Islamic State (ISIS or ISIL) also relies upon criminal enterprises to fuel its terrorist campaign and insurgency. Oil smuggling, kidnapping, human trafficking, and extortion round out their repertoire.[24] *Boko Haram*, another insurgent entity liked to al-Qaeda, also relies upon criminal enterprises for funding. In addition to raiding villages, kidnapping, and human trafficking, it engages in arms trafficking and smuggling as well as fiscal and cybercrime, and drug trafficking.[25] Elephant poaching for the illicit ivory trade also funds insurgents such as *al Shabaab* and the Lord's Liberation Army. These groups control and tax the smuggling operations within their areas of control and link with transnational criminal enterprises that operate the global illicit market flows.[26]

Interpenetration and co-option among gangs, cartels, and state officials (elected officials, including mayors, police, judges, military personnel, and intelligence officers) is the final variation of convergence. Here corrupted officials either orchestrate or support hybrid networks that enable criminals to capture or co-opt the state (or parts of the state). Examples of this convergence have been seen in Mexico, Brazil, Central America, and South Asia. Here the toxic mix is fueled by corruption and allows the maximum extraction of resources and wealth under the protection of corrupted officials resulting in impunity. The operational expertise of the gangsters, combined with the violent skills of terrorists, protected by corrupt state officials enable both criminal and political ends—whichever is desired at the specific time.[27]

The disappearance and likely murder of 43 *normalistas* (students) in Iguala led to the arrest of the city's mayor and his wife for ordering the atrocity in connection with the *Guerreros Unidos* cartel. Corrupt local police are also implicated and there have been allegations that both federal police and the military may be involved (although the state denies that link).[28] The interaction between violence, corruption, and organized crime has the potential to erode state solvency (capacity plus legitimacy) and reconfigure states.[29]

Intelligence and Law Enforcement Challenges

Understanding and addressing the convergence of transnational crime and terrorism (which must also include the role of corruption)[30] pose many difficulties for states. The first challenge is actually a basic intelligence challenge. Because there are a diverse range of occult groups linked in novel and rapidly changing, adaptive ways developing a collection strategy, plan, and capacity is complicated and subject to bureaucratic and budgetary inertia. Specialty analysts familiar with the groups may not be readily available and it might take time to develop capacity. Once the capacity is developed the group-network configuration is likely to have morphed. The remaining challenges are structural, and conceptual as well as bureaucratic.

The major challenge set involves competition. There is competition for intelligence, power, and bureaucratic standing within intelligence services and intelligence components of police. At national levels, the intelligence services compete with rival intelligence services as well as allied intelligence services in addition to the intelligence capacity of their rivals (and make no mistake, terrorists organize crime and gangs conduct intelligence operations). This intergovernmental rivalry also exists within states (national) as federal and state (provincial) and local agencies (intelligence agencies, police agencies, and fusion centers) vie for budget and recognition.

This fragmentation is a consequence of both politics and bureaucratic fiefdoms. It can be overcome, but the steady state is competition. Similar fragmentation and competition exists within agencies. For example within a single police agency different units all address separate components of threat convergence. A major city police department will have a patrol force that deals with crimes as they occur; a gangs unit to investigate gang crimes; a homicide unit that investigates murders; an organized crime unit that deals with the mafia; and narcotic units that deal with drug trafficking. A separate intelligence and crime analysis units, as well as staff seconded to a fusion center or terrorism early warning group are also likely to co-exist and compete for resources and personnel. These are within one agency. Often a precinct next door to another precinct experiencing similar gang crimes will have a delayed situational awareness of current and emerging trends.

This is exacerbated when additional police agencies are added to the mix. When supranational agencies (such as Europol or Interpol) enter the equation things get more complicated, but the additional scope of knowledge is valuable and mitigates some of the fragmentation.

Beyond interagency and intergovernmental complications, there are conceptual issues that make developing intelligence to address hybrid threats difficult. Most police agencies emphasize arrests so case support for individual cases takes precedence over operational (multi-case, multi-area) and strategic analysis, and indications and warning. The pressure is to make arrests and solve crimes, and resources are allocated to support this bias. A similar pressure is faced with addressing current intelligence over future potentials (early warning and strategic foresight).

Fusion centers (including terrorism early warning groups) were developed to address these challenges. These developments have enabled better co-ordination among agencies, but since each center has a unique signature and focus much of the fusion emphasizes dissemination of finished intelligence products developed at national levels. Some fusion centers address all crimes and hazards; others focus largely on criminal intelligence and case support. Fusion can and should exist at all stages of the intelligence cycle and much benefit could accrue as individual fusion and terrorism early warning centers are linked into networks that facilitate meta-analysis and the "co-production of intelligence" with each node contributing to insight, expertise, and area, and/or disciplinary knowledge.[31] This type of distributed police-intelligence (security service) collaboration—known as "global metropolitan policing"—could be a valuable tool for address threat convergence among terrorists and transnational criminal actors.[32]

Analytical Approaches for Hybrid Threats

As stated distributed intelligence networks emphasizing meta-analysis and "co-production of intelligence" rather than simple information sharing may help overcome the bureaucratic and conceptual obstacles (bias on current operations, arrests, and case support) to developing actionable intelligence and context on hybrid threats. These approaches require interdisciplinary analytical teams that focus on "geo-social" analysis. Mapping criminal networks is an evolving intelligence tool. Key elements of this tool[33] set are social network analysis including:

- mapping illicit networks (network configuration);
- mapping key hubs and actors by relationship;
- mapping enablers, fixers, facilitators;
- mapping illicit trade flows (smuggling, trafficking);
- mapping illicit financial transactions (investments, expenditures, money laundering) and identifying illicit financial hubs.

Mapping and discerning the function and relationship of various actors in illicit networks requires all-source intelligence—including human intelligence (HUMINT), communications intelligence (COMINT), measures and signals intelligence (MASINT), geospatial intelligence (GEOINT), criminal intelligence (CRIMINT), etc.

Identity Intelligence (i2)

A specific tool that has the potential to bridge the intelligence gaps faced with threat convergence and hybrid criminal–terrorist threats is "Identity Intelligence (i2)." i2 exploits digital space to gain an understanding of an opposing force (OPFOR), in this case, gangs/criminals, insurgents, and terrorists. Digital media include cell phones and social media (internet communications technology—ICT).

i2 is a subset of geospatial intelligence that supports investigation and intelligence by providing context and meaning which helps link actors and suggests both trends and potentials, and capabilities and intentions. It can help answer *who*, *what*, *where*, *when*, *why*, and sometimes *how*. It synthesizes the traditional INTs and adds content analysis, social network analysis, link analysis and other emerging cyber exploitation tools. Understanding social networking sites (SNS) that are used by criminals, gangs, and anarchists for internal communications, recruitment, and information operations (intimidation, shaping turf, and environment) is a key component of i2.[34] Each individual post at a SNS is a unique transaction with a potential signature that can provide indicators and context (This is part of the Transaction Analysis Cycle—Figure 1—developed by Sullivan.).[35]

Figure 1: Transaction analysis cycle

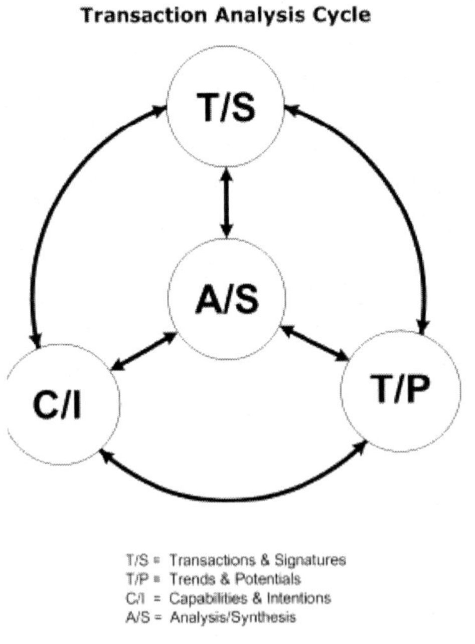

Source: *John P. Sullivan, "Terrorism early warning and co-production of counter-terrorism intelligence," paper presented to Canadian Association for Security and Intelligence Studies (CASIS), 20th Anniversary International Conference, Montreal, Quebec, Canada, October 21, 2005; available at https://www.academia.edu/927364/Terrorism_early_warning_and_co-production_of_counterterrorism_intelligence*

Unconventional media can also form part of i2 for hybrid threats. This includes graffiti (i.e., *narcomensajes* and *narcopintas*) and tattoos. These new media are essentially messaging about who the actors are and what they intend to do (or have done). Tattoos show affiliations, allegiance, fealty, position/role in hierarchy, and past actions. Deception is also a component of i2, as deception (including "burner phones," antiforensic software, GPS jammers, etc.) is frequently employed by criminal and terrorist actors to mask their activities.

The goal of i2 can be summarized as **AC²E**: *Attribution* (who is it/who did it); *Connections* (nodes, position); *Context* (what does it mean in relationship to everything else?); *Exploitation* (what can we do with it?).

Conclusion

Contemporary security threats involve the convergence of criminal and terrorist actors. Gangs, cartels, mafias, insurgents, and corrupt government officials collude and interact within an illicit space of flows.[36] These convergent threats pose security challenges at a variety of levels from gang-infested neighborhoods (failed communities or no-go zones) spanning a few blocks through entire contested zones (such as *favelas* in Brazil parts of Chihuahua, Tamaulipas, Guerrero, and Michoacán and San Pedro Sula in Honduras). These groups provide unique challenges (violence and insecurity) individually and complex challenges when they come together in alliances or in transactional operations. Corruption and violence form part of this landscape and need to be mapped.

Developing an intelligence capacity to understand these hybrid networks requires interaction among police, intelligence (and security services), and the military and civil government. It also requires interaction with a range of nongovernmental actors that provide medical, social, and humanitarian services. Intelligence approaches like distributed meta-analysis "co-production of intelligence" and the transaction analysis cycle along with expanded use of i2 are potential tools for improving intelligence to address the convergence of criminal and terrorist threats.

Notes

[1] Gary I. Wilson and John P. Sullivan, "On Gangs, Crime, and Terrorism," *Defense and the National Interest*, February 28, 2007, http://www.academia.edu/1606348/On_Gangs_Crime_and_Terrorism.
[2] Nils Gilman, Jesse Goldhhammer, and Steven Weber, eds., *Deviant Globalization: Black Market Economy in the 21st Century* (New York: Bloomsbury Academic, 2011).
[3] Michael Miklaucic, and Jacqueline Brewer, eds., *Convergence: Illicit Networks and National Security in the Age of Globalization* (Washington, DC: National Defense University Press, 2013).
[4] Martin van Creveld, *The Transformation of War* (New York: The Free Press, 1991).
[5] William S. Lind, Keith Nightingale, John F. Schmitt, Joseph W. Sutton and Gary I. Wilson, "The Changing Face of War: Into the Fourth Generation," *Marine Corps Gazette* 73 (10) (October 1989): 22-26.
[6] Joseph S. Nye, "The Future of Force," *Project Syndicate*, February 5, 2015, http://www.project-syndicate.org/commentary/modern-warfare-defense-planning-by-joseph-s—nye-2015-02#Hj6VzOU92S60czVJ.99.

[7] See John P. Sullivan, "Third generation Street Gangs: Turf, Cartels and Netwarriors," *Transnational Organized Crime* 3 (2): 95-108; John P. Sullivan, "Gangs, Hooligans, and Anarchists: The Vanguard of Netwar in the Streets," in *Networks and Netwars: The Future of Terror, Crime, and Militancy*, eds. John Arquilla, and David Ronfeldt (Santa Monica: RAND, 2001), 99-126; Robert J. Bunker and John P. Sullivan, *Studies in Gangs and Cartels* (New York: Routledge, 2013). For detailed discussion of gang dynamics.
[8] See Robert J. Bunker and John P. Sullivan, "Cartel Evolution Revisited: Third Phase Cartel Potentials and Alternative Futures in Mexico," [Special Issue: Narcos Over the Border: Gangs, Cartels, Mercenaries and the Invasion of America.] *Small Wars & Insurgencies* 21 (1): 30-54, doi: 10.1080/09592310903561379; Robert J. Bunker, "Criminal (Cartel & Gang) Insurgencies in Mexico and the Americas: What You Need to Know, Not What You Want to Hear," Testimony before the House Foreign Affairs Subcommittee on the Western Hemisphere at the Hearing 'Has Merida Evolved? Part One: The Evolution of Drug Cartels and the Threat to Mexico's Governance,'" September 13, 2011, http://archives.republicans.foreignaffairs.house.gov/112/bun091311.pdf.
[9] John P. Sullivan and Robert J. Bunker, *Mexico's Criminal Insurgency: A Small Wars Journal-El Centro Anthology* (Bloomington: iUniverse, 2012).
[10] See John P. Sullivan, "Narco-Cities: Mexico and Beyond," *Small Wars Journal* March 31, 2014, http://smallwarsjournal.com/print/15483.
[11] See Douglas Farah, *Transnational Organized Crime, Terrorism, and Criminalized States in Latin America: An Emerging Tier-One National Security Priority* (Carlisle Barracks: Strategic Studies Institute, US Army War College, 2012).
[12] See John P. Sullivan, "Transnational Gangs: The Impact of Third Generation Gangs in Central America," *Air & Space Power Journal (Spanish Edition)*, 2008, http://www.airpower.maxwell.af.mil/apjinternational/apj-s/2008/2tri08/sullivaneng.htm; John P. Sullivan, "Maras Morphing: Revisiting Third Generation Gangs," *Global Crime* 7 (3–4) (August–November 2006): 487-504. For additional discussion of *maras* and 3 GEN Gangs.
[13] John P. Sullivan and Samuel Logan, "MS-13 Leadership: Networks of Influence," *The Counter Terrorist* 3 (4) (August/September 2010): 46, http://digital.ipcprintservices.com/display_article.php?id=428186.
[14] John P. Sullivan, "La Eme (Mexican Mafia)," in *Encyclopedia of Street Crime in America*, vol. 12, ed. Jeffrey Ian Ross (Thousand Oaks, CA: SAGE Publications, Inc., 2013), 236-237, doi: http://dx.doi.org/10.4135/9781452274461.n97.
[15] John P. Sullivan and Adam Elkus, "Los Zetas and MS-13: Nontraditional Alliances," in *CTC Sentinel* (West Point: Combating Terrorism Center, 2012), https://www.ctc.usma.edu/posts/los-zetas-and-ms-13-nontraditional-alliances.
[16] John P. Sullivan, "The Barrio Azteca, Los Aztecas Network," The Counter Terrorist 6 (2) (April/May 2013), http://www.academia.edu/3246070/The_Barrio_Azteca_Los_Aztecas_Network.
[17] John P. Sullivan and Samuel Logan, "La Línea: Network, Gang, and Mercenary Army," *FARC* 4 (4) (August/September 2011), http://www.academia.edu/1123636/La_L%C3%ADnea_Network_gang_and_mercenary_army.
[18] Luis Chaparro, "Sirven 10 Pandillas de EP a Cárteles Mexicanos," *Norte Digital*, February 7, 2015, http://nortedigital.mx/sirven-10-pandillas-de-ep-a-carteles-mexicanos/.
[19] John P. Sullivan, "Transnational Crime," in *The Handbook of Global Security Policy*, eds. Mary Kaldor, and Iavor Rangelov (Oxford: Wiley Blackwell, 2014), chap. 9.
[20] See John Dickie, *Blood Brotherhoods: A History of Italy's Three Mafias* (New York: Public Affairs, 2014).
[21] See Elizabeth Bennett, "Time for India to Take Down Dawood Ibrahim," *The Diplomat*, November 4, 2014, http://thediplomat.com/2014/11/time-for-india-to-take-down-dawood-ibrahim/; Bill Roggio, "Dawood Ibrahim, al Qaeda, and the ISI," Threat Matrix blog at *Long War Journal*, January 7, 2010, http://www.longwarjournal.org/threat-matrix/archives/2010/01/dawood_ibrahim_al_qaeda_and_th.php.
[22] See Douglas Farah, "Terrorist Groups in Latin America: The Changing Landscape," *InSight Crime*, April 7, 2014, http://www.insightcrime.org/news-analysis/terrorist-groups-in-latin-america-the-changing-landscape.
[23] Of course the significance and depth of connection is subject to debate. See Victor Asal, H. Brinton Milward and Eric W. Schoon, "When Terrorists Go Bad: Analyzing Terrorist Organizations' Involvement

in Drug Smuggling," *International Studies Quarterly*, November 20, 2014, doi: 10.1111/isqu.12162; Vanda Felbab-Brown, *Shooting Up: Counterinsurgency and the War on Drugs* (Washington, DC: Brookings Institution Press, 2009). For a good review of the issue.

[24] "How ISIL Gets Its Money-Donations, Oil Smuggling, Kidnapping, Extortion," *Sputnik News*, February 7, 2015, http://sputniknews.com/analysis/20150207/1017945720.html#ixzz3RDJDI2qm. At its peak ISIS was believed to have earned $3M per day from its illicit activities, which included controlling as many as 11 oil fields in enclaves of Syria and Iraq. See Associated Press, "ISIS makes $3M per day from oil smuggling, human trafficking," *New York Post*, September 15, 2014, http://nypost.com/2014/09/15/isis-makes-3m-per-day-from-oil-smuggling-human-trafficking/.

[25] Louise Shelly, "Disrupt Boko Haram Business Strategy: Column," *USA Today*, May 22, 2014, http://www.usatoday.com/story/opinion/2014/05/22/boko-haram-kidnap-schoolgirls-military-finance-column/9454821/.

[26] See for example Perry Chiaramonte, "Terrorist Groups Fuel Rise in Violent Elephant Poaching in Central Africa," *Fox News*, February 8, 2015, http://www.foxnews.com/world/2015/02/08/guerrila-poaching-extremist-groups-violent-methods-leading-to-higher-slaughter/.

[27] In Pakistan and India D-Company has linked with Pakistan's ISI (Inter Service Intelligence) and *jihadi* elements, including al-Qaeda to conduct operations; see Bill Rogio, "Dawood Ibrahim, al Qaeda, and the ISI,"

[28] See Alma Guillermoprieto, "Mexico: 'We are Not Sheep to Be Killed'," *New York Review of Books* (Blog), November 5, 2014, http://www.nybooks.com/blogs/nyrblog/2014/nov/05/mexico-not-sheep-to-be-killed/; Ioan Grillo, "The Apparent Massacre of Dozens of Students Exposes the Corruption at the Heart of Mexico," *Time*, October 10, 2014, http://time.com/3490853/mexico-massacre-students-police-cartel-corruption/.

[29] The process here is often Co-opted State Reconfiguration (CStR) rather than State capture (StC). See John P. Sullivan, "How Illicit Networks Impact Sovereignty," in *Convergence: Illicit Networks and National Security in the Age of Globalization*, eds. Michael Miklaucic, and Jacqueline Brewer (Washington, DC: National Defense University Press, 2013), chap. 10; Luis Jorge Garay Salamanca and Eduardo Salcedo-Albarán, *Narcotráfico, corruption y Estados: Cómo las redes ilícitas han reconfigurado las instituciones en Colombia, Guatemala y México* (Mexico City: Debate, 2012).

[30] See especially Louise I. Shelly, "The Unholy Trinity: Transnational Crime, Corruption, and Terrorism," *Brown Journal of International Affairs* 11 (2) (2005): 101-111.

[31] See John P. Sullivan and James J. Wirtz, "Terrorism Early Warning and Counterterrorism Intelligence," *International Journal of Intelligence and CounterIntelligence* 21 (1): 13-25, doi: 10.1080/08850600701648686.

[32] James J. Wirtz and John P. Sullivan, "Global Metropolitan Policing: An Emerging Trend in Intelligence Sharing," *Homeland Security Affairs* 5 (May 2009), Article 4, https://www.hsaj.org/articles/103.

[33] See for example Khail Goga and Eduardo Salcedo-Albarán, "A Network of Violence: Mapping a Criminal Gang Network in Cape Town," Paper 271, Institute of Security Studies, November 28, 2014, http://www.issafrica.org/publications/papers/a-network-of-violence-mapping-a-criminal-gang-network-in-cape-town.

[34] See John P. Sullivan, "Cartel Info Ops: Power and Counter-power in Mexico's Drug War," *MountainRunner*, November15, 2010, http://mountainrunner.us/2010/11/cartel_info_ops_power_and_counter-power_in_mexico_drug_war/#.VNhalcZKKLE.

[35] See John P. Sullivan "Intelligence Co-Production and Transaction Analysis for Counterterrorism and Counter-netwar," in *Terrorism Early Warning: 10 Years of Achievement in Fighting Terrorism and Crime*, eds. John P. Sullivan, and Alain Bauer (Los Angeles: Los Angeles County Sheriff's Department, 2008), 35-43, https://www.academia.edu/1115115/Terrorism_Early_Warning_10_Years_of_Achievement_in_Fighting_Terrorism_and_Crime.

[36] On the "space of flows" see Manuel Castells, *The Informational City: Economic Restructuring and Urban Development* (Oxford: Wiley-Blackwell, 1992); Willem van Schendel, and Itty Abraham, eds., *Illicit Flows and Criminal Things: States, Borders, and the Other Side of Globalization* (Bloomington: Indiana University Press, 2005).

Advocating Balance in Penal Law and Penal Procedure

Maéla Gueguen[A]

In January 2015, the newspaper *La Provence* revealed the existence of a Facebook page which painted a stark portrait of prison conditions. Under the name "MDR o Baumettes," prisoners of the Marseilles penitentiary had posted photos and videos that bore unequivocal witness to the state of discipline and security within this establishment: blocks of hash on the beds, banknotes brandished like in Las Vegas, the laughing faces of prisoners hanging out on the gangways, some smoking shishas, others showing off their muscles in the exercise yard—it could not have been more clear that the prisoners were now running the place. Two days later, a new Facebook account run by prisoners in Nice was unveiled.

Today, prisons are facing hard times. Yet a prison sentence is only the punishment of a particular time period, and its meaning has varied over the centuries. Plato conceived of justice as a "medicine for wickedness" (*Gorgias*). Hegel maintained that punishment is a right of the criminal, whose reasonable will can only welcome the negation of his or her indignity. The new millennium has marked the passage from one extreme to another: from a world in which everything was penitence, in which one had to continually punish oneself, to another world, the current one, sorely afflicted by "penalphobia."

Daring to punish when it must be done does not mean renouncing the values and achievements of a free society. Quite the contrary, it contributes toward revitalizing and reinforcing that society: the more secure society, the more space it can then leave for freedom. The condition of doing so is for justice to combine rigor with a measured approach, rediscover its punitive function, and repress the transgression of the rules of fair conduct in a manner commensurate with the degree and gravity of the breach committed.

Although Article 6 of the European Convention of Human Rights guarantees the right to a fair trial, Article 5 of the same convention proclaims the right to freedom and security. One cannot take precedence over the other. However, the weaknesses and deficiencies of our judicial system prevent us from attaining this balance. It is therefore necessary to make law and penal procedure move in the direction of a greater realism and a greater efficacy, while preserving the strong guarantee of human rights and fundamental liberties that is characteristic of the French judicial system, and that represents the foundation of our democracy.

[A] Magistrate, Administrator in the Senate

doi: 10.18278/ijc.3.2.8

The credibility of the judicial institution is at stake here. The work of justice has lost its efficacy to such an extent that the new guarantees granted to the defense have become counterproductive: by placing so much emphasis on rights, one runs the risk of being overwhelmed by individual deviant behaviors, and of having to question the fundamental rights that found the social contract. Without the freedom to live in security (I), living in freedom can offer no security (II). The choices that national representatives make in relation to the applicable rules are crucial in this regard.

I. The Freedom to Live in Security

The Declaration of the Rights of Man and of the Citizen consecrates the inalienable and sacred character of the right to security. Originally intended as a protection against arbitrary detention, the latter has gradually become a collective right in regard to the individual: the state must be the guarantor of collective security against individual deviancies. Nowadays we recognize a "right to feel that one can live in security." Although the efficacy of investigation (A) and the efficacy of sentencing (B) are not sufficient in themselves to ensure the security of citizens, they are nevertheless a guarantee of, and a condition for, that security.

A: Effective Investigation, a Guarantee of the Right to Security

The slow pace of justice is a result of unnecessary complexities. Yet it wouldn't take a great deal of audacity to make investigation more effective. Consider the following points. . .

At the time of writing, a time when we speak of the internationalization of crime, of organized crime, of widespread targets, of cyber-cells, an investigator only has jurisdiction "within the territorial limits wherein he or she exerts his or her usual functions." In France, investigators have only recently been permitted to proceed with their investigations in neighboring counties [*départements*]. Why not authorize investigators to pursue their work throughout the national territory, or permit the prosecutor to call in an investigating officer with the appropriate territorial jurisdiction directly, just as a judge can?

Is the obligation to advise the prosecutor "without delay" when a suspect has been placed into police custody really reasonable when multiple, and sometimes turbulent, inquiries are underway, when a search could be carried out right away, or, more simply, when the place of arrest is a long way from the police station? No one believes that the prosecutor is sitting patiently next to his or her fax machine, just waiting to be advised of the next arrest, from sunset to sunrise. . . . To advise the prosecutor "within a reasonable time given the nature of the investigation" would guarantee the rights of the person in custody just as well.

Another procedural incongruity: the procedure for public intoxication was designed to protect the impenitent from himself or herself, by preventing any harm to his or her person. No hearing can take place during the time necessary to sober up, yet if the offender is subsequently arrested, this sobering-up period is discounted from their time in custody. This can hardly be justified; but if it were shortened by several hours, the measure would no longer be effective.

Continuing our indictment of the French law of investigation, the law of August 15, 2014 "on the individualizing of sentencing and reinforcing the efficacy of penal sanctions" has made it impossible to compel a person placed in custody for a contravention or an offence that is not punishable by imprisonment to appear before a court. Concretely speaking, an individual who commits violence against another causing him seven days of total incapacity to work is now free to decide not to respond to a summons from the police or gendarmes, or from the court. Would it not be desirable to restore the ability to issue said individual with an order of appearance?

The defect is always hidden where we least expect it. In regard to video-conferencing, for example, the law of March 14, 2011 makes its use dependent on the consent of the detained person. No time period is given in order to reach this agreement. However, as we know, discussions relating to detention cannot take place without the presence of a lawyer, who must be summoned at latest five business days before adversarial proceedings begin. Through various underhanded maneuvers, certain lawyers make their objection to video-conferencing known the evening before, or the very morning of, the trial—that is, at a time when it is no longer possible to summon them again. Since transport for the detained person cannot be organized at such short notice, the interested parties are automatically released. . . .

Finally, the efficacy of investigations demands that we take measures against the congestion of the investigating courts. To this day, numerous procedures result in referral to an investigating judge when certain—minimal—investigative procedures have not been carried out, but where the gravity of the matter prohibits the freeing of the person in custody. Indeed, it is often a matter of awaiting an expert report, since certain technical operations cannot be carried out within the custodial period. These various operations are generally carried out promptly, but then all the formal requirements of trial must be played out fully, with a whole cohort of unavoidable delays and obligatory procedures. After a few weeks in detention, the person indicted comes back under court supervision, and is finally judged some months, or even one or two years, later. Under these conditions, why not create a new regime of investigation, in which the prosecutor would retain control of the procedure, but could petition the liberties and detention judge for the provisional detention of the person indicted for a limited time (for a month, for example, renewable once).[1] The rights of the defense would be preserved by virtue of the guarantees pertaining to pre-trial detention in connection with a judicial investigation.

---

[1] Such a system already exists in some European countries—in particular in Germany, where the investigation is directed by a public prosecutor. Pre-trial detention—ordered by a special judge at the request of the prosecutor—can last up to six months (its duration can even be extended if a specific difficulty, an unusually extended investigation, or another important motive justify it). In Italy and Denmark, it is also the public prosecutor who requests pre-trial detention and controls the time of detention.

But however effective it might be, investigation is nothing without equally effective sentencing.

B: Effective Sentencing, a Condition of the Right to Security

Seventy-five percent of French people agree that "justice is not working," and the press does not hesitate to echo this sentiment. Here are a few extracts:

> The court found the two accused guilty of all three offences, namely aggravated theft and two attempted thefts. . . . Haron O., who had previous convictions, was given 4 years with an arrest warrant. But the youth was not led out flanked by two policemen; he had already left by the time the judgment was announced. "Already left" a courthouse from which, at the moment of being sentenced, one can leave at will, under the nose of magistrates looking helplessly.[2]

That is assuming they could actually have done something about it. . . . Under current law, nothing allows the magistrate to stop the flight of a defendant appearing freely before the criminal court. When it comes to a deliberation at the Assize Court, the presiding judge enjoins the accused not to leave the courtroom during the time of deliberation, and asks the head of security to ensure compliance with this instruction. The introduction of a similar authority at criminal courts would enhance the credibility of the institution.

Yet formal changes cannot fix fundamental flaws. The discontinuation of the automatic revocation of suspended sentences [*sursis simples*] when a further offence is committed, as established by the law of August 15, 2014, has effectively rendered 120,000 sentences per year fictional. Legal experience has already shown the highly debatable effect of suspended sentences. Under this regime, numerous defendants now have to appear in court again to maintain that they were never convicted. With automatic revocation abolished, judges sometimes forget to pronounce on the revocation, and indeed often refuse to proceed with it, considering that it would amount to a kind of "double jeopardy." Or, better yet, they reduce the imprisonment they wish to impose in due proportion to the existing suspended sentence. The circular of December 17, 2014 added further alterations to the law, indicating that a suspended sentence passed by a collegiate court cannot be revoked by a court ruling alone. . . .

The harmony of a score cannot abide bad tuning. In penal law, we tend to make more use of flat than of sharp, to the extent that the right note is lost. As just one example, take the authority granted to the judge to pass a sentence in court.

[2] Xavier Raufer, "Justice: Chronique d'une faillite annoncée," *Le Nouvel Économiste*, last updated March 3, 2014, http://www.lenouveleconomiste.fr/justice-chronique-dune-faillite-annoncee-21746/.

Actual imprisonment, inflicted on around 16 percent of prosecutable perpetrators, remains a relatively residual response.[3] If, despite the wide range of options at his or her disposal, the judge chooses to pass such a sentence, it is indeed because he or she intends it to be effective. How then are we to understand the fact that that the judge can then go on to apply reductions and adjustments to the penalty in court—that is to say, at the very moment when passing sentence? The adjustment of the sentence must remain within the competence of the liberties and detention judge; otherwise, a penal response is scarcely intelligible.

Penal justice can suffer neither excess nor imbalance. The hope given by a sentence nearing its end may encourage convicts to change their ways. In this sense, a reduction of punishment for good behavior may make sense; but it must not become a given. Knowing from the very day of conviction that the detainee will not serve all of the time is something difficult to comprehend. We must give back some meaning to the reduction of sentences by making it depend on the "merits" of the detainee, as is the case currently with the reduction of supplementary sentences.

If the person reoffends, what sense does it make for him to continue benefitting from these reductions? One must certainly leave the hope of making amends and the chance to do so, and thus the possibility of a reduction in the penalty, but to a lesser degree.

Moreover, passing a sentence does not necessarily mean that the sentence will be served. Penalties of imprisonment for a duration less than or equal to two years—one year in the case of reoffending—are generally not served, but are subject to adjustments that weaken their meaning. Can a penalty of community work or a fine be proportionate to a penalty of six months imprisonment? Can two years imprisonment be exchanged for two years of electronic tagging at home, with the authorization to go out to collect one's children from school? It is a long time now since we believed, with Cesare Beccaria, that "the certainty of punishment, even a moderate one, will always make more of an impression than the fear of a terrible penalty if this fear is combined with the hope of impunity."

This accumulation of false notes ends up depriving the system of any and all coherence. The mechanism of conditional release [*liberation sous contrainte*], introduced by the penal reform of August 15, 2014, marks a departure in the logic of the adjustment of sentences. Prior to the introduction of this option, adjustments had to be solicited by the convict. The latter was thus encouraged to initiate steps toward release, to seek a job, to compensate the plaintiff, so as to demonstrate a record of good behavior likely to inspire a judge's confidence in the success of the requested adjustment. With controlled release, this is not at all the case. Once the convict has carried out two thirds of his penalty, the judge for the execution of sentences is obliged to examine the situation in the Committee for the Execution of Sentences—that is to say, during an "administrative" meeting of the judge and rehabilitation professionals, without the

[3] Source: Report of the *Observatoire national de la délinquance et des réponses pénales* for 2014.

presence of the convict and without his even having requested such a consideration. It is a commonplace that we need to make sentencing meaningful again—but shouldn't we also make the adjustment of sentences meaningful as well?

In 1980, Minister of Justice Alain Peyrefitte gave us the now celebrated phrase: "security is the first freedom." Pierre Mauroy responded, a year later, that "the first security is freedom." Apparently incompatible and yet indissociable, these two objectives transcend their apparent opposition in the best possible way: one will always be the condition of the other.

II. The Security to Live in Freedom

Security is one of the conditions for the exercise of individual and collective freedoms alike. For this exercise of liberty, it is necessary for norms to be secure; without legal certainty, without the predictability of the norm, there can be no freedom (A). However, this is not the only condition: without a working judicial system, acting in the form of a fair trial and within a reasonable time frame, citizens' rights cannot be recognized. The efficacy of the judge is thus revealed to be a condition of freedom (B).

A: The Efficacy of the Norm, a Guarantee of Freedom

How can we guarantee citizens an effective enjoyment of the fundamental right to freedom? Above all by recognizing their rights—but not just any rights: those of which they make real use. Among the myriad new rights—which issue primarily, at least in principle, from European Law—many are relatively ineffective. Others, however, deserve to be recognized.

Allowing an appeal against an indictment order, for example. At the moment, an indictment order is not a legal measure open to appeal. The judge must decide whether there are "serious and corroborated indications" that the commission of an infraction has likely taken place. This is a purely factual evaluation; he or she does not have to justify the decision. The only recourse for the concerned party is a request for the annulment of the order, which will be examined many months afterwards by the investigating chamber. This annulment does not, however, call for a reassessment of the serious and corroborated indications; it is justified by the failure to observe legal formalities essential to the validity of the order. This situation is unsatisfactory, because an indictment carries heavy consequences, particularly in the political arena, but also in business, and even for a normal citizen who may see himself or herself declared guilty in the eyes of the public. It would be a good idea to require a written, substantiated order, indicating what justifies the indictment in fact and in law, and to permit an appeal to be made against it (within a limited time frame). This measure would also have the merit of protecting judges against criticisms of arbitrariness. It would reconcile the appeal and the principle of collegiality. Finally, it would favor recourse to the status of assisted witness, which remains to this day something of a failure because it is not employed often enough.

Making appeals possible against orders of referral to the Criminal Court. Following criminal investigation, the public prosecutor takes submissions for dismissal or referral to the court, and then the judge makes the order. If the judge decides the case should be dismissed, it can be appealed by the public prosecutor. On the contrary, an order of referral cannot be appealed by the defendant, except in one case: he or she can challenge the criminal nature of the facts. The facts themselves can only be contested before the court, when the case itself is brought. Allowing appeals against an order of referral would favor an increased respect for the rights of the defense, would introduce collegiality at the stage of the assessment of charges, and would align the regime of referral to Criminal Court with that of indictment before the Assize Court.

More freedom through the recognition of new rights: this is an avenue that deserves constant exploration. However, it will not bring about more effective freedom without normative stability, without legal certainty. And legal certainty, a counterpart to the old adage *Ignorantia juris neminem excusat*, is today under considerable threat by jurisprudence.

The rules relating to the statute of limitations for state prosecutions are a fine illustration of this state of affairs. In November 2014, for example, the Cottrez affair reignited debates on the topic.[4] A mother was suspected of having killed eight of her children at birth. However, more than ten years had passed before the death of the newborns was discovered. The successive pregnancies had passed unnoticed given the mother's obesity; none of the births had been officially registered; and the bodies had remained hidden. According to the Court of Cassation, the clandestine nature of the births and deaths posed an insurmountable obstacle to prosecution. Given this fact, it was ruled that the limitation period should be regarded as beginning with the discovery of the bodies. The system is rather untenable due to the artificial and *contra legem* nature of the notions of discovery and dissimulation. The praetorian application of the rules of limitation, the result of a society of emotion, clashes with the principles of legibility and stability, the source of legal certainty and confidence in the law and its institutions.

Nevertheless, the present statute of limitations on state prosecutions does seem excessively short. It falls to legislators, rather than judges, to intervene here. If Justice wishes to live up to its values and its proper concept, we must seek a global, reasonable principle that allows for a longer statutes, albeit ones that would not vary for every single case.

Another illustration of the instability of the norm, and a far from trivial one, is the jurisprudence of the Plenary Assembly of the Court of Cassation in relation to the regularity of measures of custody.

In four orders made on April 15, 2011, the Plenary Assembly of the Court of Cassation considered custody measures not in conformity with Article 6 § 1 of the European Convention on Human Rights, on the grounds that the persons in custody

[4] Plenary Assembly of the Court of Cassation, order no. 613 (14-83.739), November 7, 2014.

did not have the assistance of a lawyer and were not notified of their right to remain silent.

The difficulty lay in determining whether this ruling regarding the non-conformity of the French legislation was effective from the time of the decision, or retroactively. The Court of Cassation made the choice to apply its jurisprudence retroactively, thus demarcating itself from the Constitutional Council. As a consequence, all custody procedures underway at the time became null and void, even when they had been conducted in conformity with the laws in force. Nothing has ever been said about the suspects who got off lightly, nor the victims whose rights were never considered. . . .

The right to freedom is at once a right to challenge (which should have its new abilities to contest crucial jurisdictional procedures recognized), the right of a citizen (who has the right to know whether he or she risks being prosecuted or not), and that of a victim (to see the directive principles of investigation preserved in such a way as to avoid seeing trial proceedings incomprehensibly abandoned). Yet even if these rights became effective, judges would still have to act effectively.

B. The Efficacy of Judges, a Condition of Freedom

There are countless complaints about the slow pace of justice. This should not, however, be blamed only on magistrates and civil servants. The action or inaction of certain auxiliaries of the legal system must also be considered. The time necessary for a trial must be time that is put to good use. This means that we ought to direct our attention towards the places where time is lost, if we want to do away with unnecessary, pointless, or wasted time. What counts is not only the quantity of time taken by a trial, but also and above all the way in which this time has been used by its various actors.

In fact, this is something that we see in the jurisprudence of the European Court of Human Rights. In order to assess the duration of judicial procedures, the latter takes into account the behavior of national authorities—in other words, the means placed at the disposal of the justice system in order to respect a reasonable timespan—the behavior of the judge—whether judges have made too many referrals, whether they have omitted to penalize inaction on the part of others—and the behavior of the parties themselves—whether they have appointed a succession of different lawyers, tabled multiple interlocutory applications, or neglected to respond to the judge's orders?

Several recommendations can be made in order to handle the time of legal proceedings more effectively:

Limiting the intervention of lawyers in substantive procedures. The presence of the lawyer when a case is referred to the proper court [déférement], made obligatory by the law of May 27, 2014, is of no help to the respondent. The lawyer may have been

---

[5] Plenary Assembly of the Court of Cassation, April 15, 2011, orders 589, 590, 591, and 592.

of some aid at the time when the latter was placed into custody, and had the chance to confer with his or her client before the hearing; the lawyer will have had access to the whole procedure. Before the public prosecutor, however, the lawyer has nothing to say, and can only listen, alongside his client, to the decision related to the direction the procedure will take. The referral of the case is a simple notification of charges and of information on the remainder of the procedure.

Giving back control of the process to judges, by giving judges control over the filing of pleadings and motions. The late filing of pleas or motions—often so as to invalidate a case—is the source of a major dysfunction for the criminal courts. The facts are simple: the defense pleads a "flawed case," not on legal but on formal grounds, and the backlog of hearings does the rest: one must then wait many months for a new hearing date. The adversarial principle is an essential guarantee of a fair trial. As such, all parties must respect it. It is rather incomprehensible, then, that the defense has the right to see the investigation file two months at least before the date of the hearing,[6] and that it is authorized to file pleas and documents right up to the last few minutes before the opening of the hearing. Under these conditions, why not impose a time limit for submitting pleas and motions to the Criminal Court—with the exception of immediate appearance—and the Police Court, with every late filing incurring the penalty of a motion of inadmissibility, unless the court makes a reasoned decision otherwise?

Respecting the requirements of the European Court, without overstepping them. Arguments drawn from the jurisprudence of the European Court of Human Rights are used with increasing frequency in political and internal judicial debate. Yet it is interesting to observe how certain people misrepresent their meaning the better to instrumentalize them and to make a case for the inevitability of the reforms they want to call for—even if this means imputing requirements to them that they do not make, at the risk of disorganizing our legal system.

At the very same moment when the endless delays and the slow pace of the justice system are vilified, recent reforms have almost automatically increased the wait time for hearings.[7] When the time between the delivery of a summons and the date of a hearing is less than two months, article 390-2 of the Code of Penal Procedure provides for a postponement of the case simply at the request of the respondent. The same requirement is posited in article 388-2 for the delivery of copies.

These arrangements overstep the exigencies of European law, which demands only

> that access is granted at least to all material evidence in the possession of the competent authorities, whether for or against suspects or accused persons, to those persons or their lawyers . . . in due time to

[6] Article 390-2 of the penal procedure code, resulting from the law of May 27, 2014.

[7] Law no. 2014–535 of May 27, 2014, transposition of directive 2012/13/UE of the European Parliament and Council, May 22, 2012 on the right to information in criminal proceedings.

> allow the effective exercise of the rights of the defense and at the latest upon submission of the merits of the accusation to the judgment of a court.[8]

Abolishing notification of the right to remain silent at a public hearing. The law of April 27, 2014 stipulates that in public hearings, the judge must remind the accused that they have the right to remain silent. We should illustrate what this means in practical terms: the usher calls the case, the respondent steps forward to the bar, and the presiding judge indicates to him or her that he or she is appearing to explain the facts, but has the right to remain silent, if he or she does not already know it! And indeed, the respondent has already been notified of the right to remain silent during the investigation stage. Worse still, at the Assize Court, where the proceedings are entirely oral, the presiding judge indicates to the accused that the jury will pronounce upon his or her guilt following the proceedings (the jurors do not have access to the investigation file), but that he or she has the right to remain silent! Similarly, a person initially found guilty who decides to interject an appeal for motives known only to himself or herself, once again, will be notified of his or her right to remain silent. And yet European Law does not call for notification of this right before a public hearing.

We must review the compromise of the law of May 14, 2011, and abolish the new obligations to notify the respondent of the right to silence before a court. Failing this, it would make sense to create an offense of perjury, and to penalize a defendant for lying at the bar. The corollary of the right to remain silent must be a prohibition on lying.[9]

Didn't Joseph Joubert say that justice without force and force without justice both lead to terrible misfortune?

---

[8] Directive 2012/13/UE of the European Parliament and Council of May 22, 2012 on the right to information in criminal proceedings: Right of access to the materials of the case, Article 7, paragraphs 2 and 3.

[9] Comparative law offers many fine examples. In the US, the crime of perjury can carry a sentence of up to five years in prison. In Spain, defendants have the obligation to respond to the judge's questions and do not have the right to lie. Prosecutions for the offence of perjury are also frequent against witnesses.

Made in United States
North Haven, CT
05 November 2026

21772481R00074